AGA Institute/PAHCS

# Gastroenterology Coding Manual

Second Edition

AGA Institute and the
Professional Association
of Healthcare Coding Specialists

AGA Institute
AGA Education, Practice and Research

PAHCS

# AGA Institute/PAHCS Gastroenterology Coding Manual

Second Edition



**AGA Institute Press**

| | |
|---|---|
| Christine B. Charlip | Division Director of Publications |
| Cindy DeLano | Production Director |
| Jennifer Halbert | Cover Design |
| Circle Graphics, Inc. | Composition |
| McNaughton & Gunn, Inc. | Printing |

**Disclaimer**

This publication provides accurate information on the subject matter covered. The publisher is not providing legal, medical, or other professional services. Reference herein to any specific commercial products, procedures, or services by trade name, trademark, manufacturer, or otherwise does not constitute or imply endorsement, recommendation, or favored status by the AGA Institute. The views and opinions of the author(s) expressed in this publication do not necessarily state or reflect those of the AGA Institute, and they shall not be used to advertise or endorse a product.



Printed in the United States of America

12 11 10 09 08 1 2 3 4 5

ISBN 978-1-60356-002-3

For additional copies or information on licensing or translating this content, please contact:

AGA INSTITUTE PRESS
Advancing Digestive Health

4930 Del Ray Avenue
Bethesda, MD 20814-2513
www.gastro.org/publications

# Contents

# Acknowledgments

The *AGA INSTITUTE/PAHCS Gastroenterology Coding Manual* was written by the AGA Institute's Center for GI Practice Management and Economics and the Professional Association of Healthcare Coding Specialists. Special recognition goes to Cecile Katzoff, MGA, CGCS, Director of the AGA Center for GI Practice Management and Economics, for her work in bringing together these two groups.

We gratefully acknowledge the work of the AGA Institute Practice Management and Economics Committee for their review of this manual, especially James Aisenberg, MD; Peter S. Donaldson, MBA; and Lawrence R. Kosinski, MD. Committee Chair Joel V. Brill, MD, AGAF, in particular, brought his expertise to bear on this manual and improved it substantially for the second edition. In addition, we recognize and extend many thanks to Cecile Katzoff, MGA, CGCS; Anne Marie Bicha, CPC, CGCS; Jennifer Conte, CGCS; and Kathleen Mueller, RN, CPC, CCS-P, CMSCS, PCS, for their expert review and detailed comments.

# Introduction

The *AGA Institute/PAHCS Gastroenterology Coding Manual* was created to provide the gastroenterology coder with the essential elements of gastroenterology coding in an easy-to-access format. For experienced coders, the material will refresh and reinforce your coding skills, providing confidence that you have retained a vast amount of knowledge over a long period of time. For the coder with less experience, the material will provide a resource for coding that will clarify previously complex conventions. This text assumes the reader has some knowledge of the health care field and of coding structure.

The first part of the *Gastroenterology Coding Manual* is specialty-centered and includes coding scenarios specific to the gastroenterology practice. Note that this information is organized by organ system and by procedure rather than by code family. The second part of the manual is based on coding conventions and general coding skills. It is highly recommended that you also use your ICD-9-CM, CPT, and HCPCS books as additional coding sources and read the guidelines and conventions for each chapter.

This text is a synopsis of the tools of our trade and is intended to help guide you in your knowledge of coding rules, conventions, and helpful coding hints. The dual goals of the American Gastroenterological Association (AGA) Institute and the Professional Association of Healthcare Coding Specialists are to assist you in acquiring the knowledge to be a successful Gastroenterology Specialty Coder and to prepare you for the Gastroenterology Certification Examination.

Please note that this manual contains material derived from various reliable sources that was believed to be current and accurate at the time of printing. However, coding is a work in progress. Not only do changes occur on a daily basis, but "experts" often disagree on the interpretation of the coding rules. Therefore, AGA Institute and PAHCS disclaim any and all responsibility for actions taken in relation to the enclosed material and strongly recommend consultation with reliable coding sources for guidance in specific circumstances.

In addition, updates and revisions to the *AGA Institute/PAHCS Gastroenterology Coding Manual*, including annually updated CPT codes, are posted at the following site:

**http://www.gastro.org/CodingUpdates**

Please check this site for important updates that will help you better use this manual.

# Procedure Coding

chapter 1

# Gastroenterology Coding Principles

## I. General Guidelines for Endoscopy

The following are examples of procedures that can be performed during an endoscopy:

- Collection of specimens by brushing or washing
- Biopsy (the removal of a tissue specimen, part of a lesion, or the entire lesion using cold biopsy forceps)
- Removal of a foreign body
- Directed submucosal injection of substances
- Decompression of a volvulus
- Endoscopic sphincterotomy/papillotomy
- Pressure measurement of the sphincter of Oddi
- Endoscopic retrograde removal of calculi from the biliary and/or pancreatic ducts
- Endoscopic lithotripsy
- Insertion of a nasobiliary or nasopancreatic drainage tube
- Banding of varices and hemorrhoids
- Sclerotherapy of varices and hemorrhoids
- Endoscopic mucosal resection of a lesion
- Endoscopic ultrasound (EUS)
- Ultrasound guided fine needle aspiration (FNA) or transmural biopsy
- Balloon dilation (dilatation) of a stricture or narrowing of the lumen
- Insertion of a guidewire followed by dilation over the guidewire
- Drainage of a pancreatic pseudocyst
- Insertion of a plastic stent or tube
- Transendoscopic placement of a intraluminal tube or catheter
- Hot biopsy or bipolar cautery removal of a lesion or polyp
- Snare removal of lesion or polyp
- Ablation of a lesion not amenable to treatment by hot biopsy, cautery, or snare
- Control of bleeding by any method

- Delivery of thermal energy to the lower esophageal sphincter
- Suturing of the esophagogastric junction
- Placement of a percutaneous endoscopic gastrostomy (PEG) or percutaneous endoscopic jejunostomy (PEJ) tube

When two or more distinct procedures are performed at different sites during the same session, it is appropriate to separately report these procedures with the 59 modifier, when bundled by National Correct Coding Initiative (NCCI) edits and identified with a modifier "2."

## II. Endoscopic Services Guidelines and Bundling Policies

The following guideline/policy is found in Chapter VI in the introduction to the NCCI available at the Center for Medicare and Medical Services (CMS) Web site: http://www.cms.hhs.gov/NationalCorrectCodInitEd/. Look under the NCCI Policy Manual for Part B Medicare Carriers.

Additional procedures that may be performed during an endoscopy (e.g., venous access and/or injections, noninvasive oximetry, anesthesia provided by the physician) are considered an integral part of the endoscopy and as such are not separately billed.

The following are guidelines for endoscopy:

1. When a diagnostic endoscopy is performed in conjunction with endoscopic therapeutic services, the appropriate CPT code to use is the most comprehensive endoscopy code describing the service performed. If the same therapeutic endoscopy service is performed repeatedly (e.g., polyp removal) in the same area, only one CPT code is reported with one unit of service. If different therapeutic services are performed and are not adequately described by a more comprehensive CPT code, for example, a polypectomy from the descending colon and biopsies from the ascending colon, the appropriate codes can be designated in accordance with the multiple endoscopy rule.
2. When a diagnostic endoscopy is followed by a surgical endoscopy, the diagnostic endoscopy is considered part of the surgical endoscopy and is not to be reported separately.
3. Gastroenterological tests included in codes 91000–91299 are frequently complementary to endoscopic procedures. Esophageal and gastric washings for cytology are described as part of upper endoscopy (43235); therefore, codes 91000 (esophageal intubation) and 91105 (gastric intubation) should not be reported separately when performed as part of an upper endoscopic procedure.
4. When a small intestine endoscopy is performed as a necessary part of a procedure, only the most comprehensive code describing the service performed is reported. For instance, when a biopsy of the jejunum is performed in which the scope has been advanced beyond the ligament of Treitz, and another biopsy is taken of the antrum of the stomach, the most extensive endoscopy procedure, code 44361, should be reported, not 44361 and 44239. Performance of an esophagogastroduodenoscopy (EGD) is inherent to the performance of small intestine endoscopy.

5. When endoscopic esophageal dilation is performed, report the appropriate endoscopic esophageal dilation code. Codes 43450–43458 are not used in addition to the endoscopy codes, even if attempted unsuccessfully prior to endoscopic dilation. Modifier 22 could be used to indicate an unusual endoscopic dilation procedure.
6. When it is necessary to perform diagnostic endoscopy of the biliary/hepatic/pancreatic system using separate approaches (e.g., biliary T-tube endoscopy and ERCP) the appropriate codes for both services may be reported. The code should include the 51 modifier, indicating multiple procedures were performed at the same session. In 2002, CMS revised the global surgical policy, stating not to bill the 51 modifier to Medicare. Although in this case no modifier needs to be added in this instance for services provided to Medicare beneficiaries, other insurers may require the 51 modifier.
7. When intubation of the gastrointestinal tract is performed (e.g., percutaneous G-tube placement), it is not appropriate to bill a separate code for tube removal. Code 43247 (endoscopic removal of foreign body) is not reported for routine removal of a therapeutic device such as a gastrostomy tube that was previously placed.
8. When an endoscopic or open procedure is performed and a biopsy is also performed, followed by excision, destruction, or removal of the biopsied lesion, the biopsy is not separately reported. Additionally:
   - When bleeding results from an endoscopic or surgical service (e.g., biopsy, polypectomy), control of bleeding at the time of service is included in the endoscopic procedure and is not reported separately.
   - Separate procedure codes for control of bleeding are not coded.
   - If it is necessary to repeat the endoscopy at a later time during the same day to control bleeding, a procedure coded for endoscopic control of bleeding may be reported with a 78 modifier, indicating that this service represents a separate return to the operating room for a related procedure during the postoperative period.
9. Only the most extensive endoscopic procedure is reported for a session. For example, if a sigmoidoscopy is completed and the physician performs a colonoscopy during the same session, only the colonoscopy is coded.
   - It is acceptable to bill for multiple services provided during an endoscopic procedure, with the exception of treating bleeding induced by the procedure.
   - These services would be reimbursed by Medicare under the multiple endoscopy payment rules. For multiple endoscopic procedures, Medicare pays the full value of the highest valued endoscopy plus the difference between the next highest procedure and the base endoscopy.
10. When a transabdominal colonoscopy (via colostomy; code 45355) and/or standard sigmoidoscopy or colonoscopy is/are performed as a necessary part of an open procedure, the endoscopic procedure(s) is/are not separately reported.
11. When moderate sedation is provided by the physician performing the endoscopy, the anesthesia services are included in the endoscopy reimbursement and are not separately billable. If it is medically necessary for a separate provider (anesthesiologist/anesthetist) to provide the anesthesia services (e.g., monitored anesthesia care), a separate service may be reported by the separate provider.

See Chapter 9 for detailed information on modifiers.

# III. Family of Codes

- All endoscopic codes are listed as families. The base code, or head of the family, is the diagnostic endoscopy and is reported when all the physician does is look and not touch. Note that the base code includes brushing or washings.
- The family members are considered the surgical endoscopies. When a surgical endoscopy is performed, the diagnostic endoscopy is considered a component of the surgical endoscopy and is not separately billable.
- More than one surgical endoscopy can be performed and can be reported as long as it was a different technique that involved a different site in the gastrointestinal tract.

# IV. More Extensive Procedures

When procedures are performed together that are basically the same or performed on the same site but are qualified by an increased level of complexity, the less extensive procedure is included in the more extensive procedure. Examples include the following:

- Simple and complex CPT codes on the same site:
  - The simple procedure is included in the complex.
- Limited and complete CPT codes on the same site:
  - The limited procedure is included in the complete.
- Superficial and deep CPT codes:
  - The superficial is included in the deep procedure.
- Intermediate and comprehensive:
  - The intermediate is included in the comprehensive.
- Incomplete and complete CPT codes on the same site
  - Incomplete is included in the complete procedure.
- External and internal CPT codes:
  - The external procedure is included in the internal.

For example, if a biopsy of a sessile polyp is performed in the transverse colon followed by ablation of the same lesion, the ablation is considered the most extensive procedure and therefore would be the only billable procedure.

# V. Endoscopy Codes

| Type of Endoscopy | Code Range |
|---|---|
| Esophagoscopy | 43200–43228 |
| Esophagogastroduodenoscopy (EGD) | 43235–43259 |
| Endoscopic retrograde cholangiopancreatography (ERCP) | 43260–43272 |
| Enteroscopy (small intestine endoscopy) | 44360–44379 |
| Ileoscopy | 44382–44383 |
| Endoscopic evaluation of pouch | 44385–44386 |
| Colonoscopy through stoma | 44388–44397 |
| Proctosigmoidoscopy | 45300–45321 |
| Sigmoidoscopy | 45330–45339 |
| Colonoscopy | 45378–45385 |
| Anoscopy | 46600–46615 |

## A. Esophagoscopy, Upper GI Endoscopy, and Enteroscopy

Some of the esophagoscopy, EGD, and enteroscopy codes contain the same descriptors. The only difference is the distance traveled through the upper GI tract. Some state Medicare contractors have Local Coverage Determination Policies for upper GI endoscopies. Please check with your individual Medicare contractor.

### *Definitions*

Esophagoscopy is limited to study of esophagus.
EGD includes study of the esophagus, stomach, and either the duodenum and/or jejunum.
Enteroscopy (push or deep enteroscopy) is small intestinal endoscopy, enteroscopy beyond second portion of duodenum, not including ileum or including ileum.

- When the pyloric channel, gastric outlet, or gastric–small intestinal anastomosis is traversed, it is described as an EGD.
- When the small intestine past the second portion of the duodenum is visualized, it is described as small intestine endoscopy or enteroscopy.
- The EGD codes should be used to describe evaluation of the patient who has undergone previous gastric surgery where there is a gastro-jejunal (e.g., Billroth II) or similar anastomosis.
- Anterograde deep enteroscopy can be coded using the enteroscopy codes. Retrograde deep enteroscopy can be coded as an unlisted procedure. (see page 26).

**43200** Parent code of esophagoscopy; diagnostic esophagoscopy.

**43235** Parent code of EGD; diagnostic EGD.

**44360** Parent code of enteroscopy/small intestine endoscopy not including ileum.

**44376** Parent code of enteroscopy/small intestine endoscopy including ileum.

- The collection of specimens by brushing or washing is included in reporting these codes.

- Brushing or washing is a separate procedure and cannot be billed with any other code in the same family.
- If a surgical endoscopy is performed during the same session, the diagnostic endoscopy is not separately reported.

**43201** Esophagoscopy with directed submucosal injection.

**43236** EGD with directed submucosal injection.

- Includes the injection of medication such as Botox, India Ink (tattooing), saline, and/or steroids. This does not include the injection of sclerosing solution or epinephrine to control bleeding. There are separate endoscopy codes for the injection of sclerosing solution for varices or epinephrine to control bleeding.
- If saline is used to elevate the lesion prior to excision, the saline injection is reported separately but may be paid according to the multiple endoscopy rule.

**43202** Esophagoscopy with biopsy.

**43239** EGD with biopsy.

**44361** Enteroscopy/small intestine endoscopy not including ileum with biopsy.

**44377** Enteroscopy/small intestine endoscopy including ileum with biopsy.

- These codes should be reported only one time regardless of the number of biopsies performed. If multiple biopsies are performed in different areas of the upper GI tract, the most extensive biopsy would be reported.
- If the same lesion is biopsied and subsequently removed during the same operative session, only the code for the removal of the lesion would be reported.
- If one lesion is biopsied and a separate lesion (from another site in the intestine) is removed during the same session by means of a separate technique other than the biopsy, it would be appropriate to report a code for the biopsy of one lesion and an additional code for the removal of the separate lesion.
- The use of the 59 modifier is essential when billing for a biopsy for one lesion and removal of a separate lesion. The modifier is added to the biopsy lesion.
- If a CLO test (test for *Helicobacter pylori*) is performed, this is correctly billed as a biopsy.

**43204 and 43205** Esophagoscopy procedures with treatment of esophageal varices.

**43243 and 43244** EGD procedures with treatment of either esophageal and/or gastric varices.

- 43204 is used to report esophagoscopy with injection sclerosis of esophageal varices.
- 43205 is used to report esophagoscopy with band ligation of esophageal varices.
- 43243 is used to report EGD with injection of sclerosing solution of esophageal or gastric varices.
- 43244 is used to report EGD with band ligation of esophageal or gastric varices.

**43215** Esophagoscopy with removal of foreign body.

**43247** EGD with removal of foreign body.

**44363** Enteroscopy/small intestine endoscopy not including ileum with removal of foreign body.

- If the procedure is performed with radiologic guidance, a separate code from the 70000 series may be reported for the radiologic supervision and interpretation.
- If fluoroscopy is utilized, code 76000, Fluoroscopy (separate procedure), up to 1 hour physician time, would be reported. The radiology codes require the 26 modifier when performed in a facility.

- As with all radiology codes, there may be a conflict if the radiologist is present or issues a report because a hard copy of the film is sent to the radiology department. Check with your physician(s) before billing the radiologic supervision and interpretation codes.

**43216** Esophagoscopy with removal of tumor(s), polyp(s), or other lesion(s) using hot biopsy forceps or bipolar cautery.

**43250** EGD with removal of tumor(s), polyp(s), or other lesion(s) using hot biopsy forceps or bipolar cautery.

**44365** Enteroscopy/small intestine endoscopy not including ileum, with removal of tumor(s), polyp(s), or other lesion(s) using hot biopsy forceps or bipolar cautery.

- Hot biopsy forceps use monopolar current, requiring the use of a grounding pad placed somewhere on the patient's body.
- Bipolar current does not require a grounding pad, as current runs simply from one portion of the tip of the device to another.

**43217** Esophagoscopy with removal of tumor(s), polyp(s), or other lesion(s) using snare.

**43251** EGD with removal of tumor(s), polyp(s), or other lesion(s) using a snare.

**44364** Enteroscopy/small intestine endoscopy not including ileum, with removal of tumor(s), polyp(s), or other lesion(s) by snare technique.

- A snare is a wire loop that is used to encircle tissue, rather than to simply grab it. This can be either a cold or hot snare.

**43228** Esophagoscopy with removal of tumor(s), polyp(s), or other lesion(s) not amenable to removal by hot biopsy, bipolar cautery, or snare.

**43258** EGD with removal of tumor(s), polyp(s), or other lesion(s) not amenable to removal by hot biopsy, bipolar cautery, or snare.

**44369** Enteroscopy/small intestine endoscopy not including ileum, with removal of tumor(s), polyp(s), or other lesion(s) not amenable to removal by hot biopsy, bipolar cautery, or snare.

- The removal of a lesion using the same technique is to be reported only once per operative session regardless of the number of lesions treated using that treatment method.
- Check the operative report carefully to verify the technique used to remove the lesion(s).
- Multiple lesions may be removed using different techniques. If different techniques are used, bill the codes that describe each technique used.
- The second, third, fourth, etc., techniques are listed with a 59 modifier to indicate a separate site within the intestine when the component code is bundled into the most comprehensive code.

**43320** Esophagoscopy with balloon dilation (less than 30 mm in diameter).

**43249** EGD with balloon dilation (less than 30 mm in diameter).

- The measurement in this code refers to the maximum diameter of the balloon itself (not the diameter of the esophagus).
- These codes describe those cases where a through-the-scope (TTS) type balloon dilator is used.
- The endoscope remains in place as a balloon-tipped catheter is passed through its instrument channel and dilation is performed as the balloon is inflated under direct endoscopic observation.

- Parenthetical notes that appear following code 43320 direct the user to 43458 for endoscopic dilation with a balloon 30 mm in diameter or larger.
- The term *French* as applied to the diameter of the balloon does not equal mm, e.g., 60 French equals 20 mm.

**43226** Esophagoscopy with insertion of a guidewire and subsequent dilation of the esophagus over the guidewire.

**43248** EGD with insertion of a guidewire and subsequent dilation of the esophagus over the guidewire.

- Includes both the insertion of the guidewire and the dilation of the esophagus.
- Involves the passage of the endoscope, after which a flexible-tipped guidewire is passed through the endoscope into the stomach. The endoscope is then withdrawn, leaving the guidewire in place.
- A series of dilators (e.g., American, Savary) are then passed over the guidewire to dilate the lumen.

**43227** Esophagoscopy with control of bleeding.

**43255** EGD with control of bleeding.

**44366** Enteroscopy/small intestine endoscopy not including ileum with control of bleeding.

**44378** Enteroscopy/small intestine endoscopy including ileum with control of bleeding.

- Bleeding can be treated by several endoscopic techniques including but not limited to the following:
  - Application of cautery with heater probe or bipolar or monopolar probe
  - Injection of vasocontrictive (e.g., epinephrine or irritant liquids) agents
  - Laser cautery
- All methods used to control bleeding are reported using the one code.

**43246** EGD with percutaneous endoscopic gastrostomy (PEG) tube placement.

- When a PEG tube is placed by two physicians, each physician reports code 43246 with the 62 modifier appended.
- When a PEG tube is removed and replaced endoscopically at the same session, use code 43246, because the removal is bundled into the insertion.

**44372** Enteroscopy/small intestine endoscopy with placement of percutaneous jejunostomy (PEJ) tube.

**44373** Enteroscopy/small intestine endoscopy with conversion of percutaneous gastrostomy (PEG) tube to percutaneous jejunostomy (PEJ) tube.

**43231** Esophagoscopy with endoscopic ultrasound (EUS).

**43237** EGD with endoscopic ultrasound (EUS) limited to the esophagus.

**43259** EGD with endoscopic ultrasound (EUS) including the esophagus, stomach, and duodenum.

- CPT instructs the physician performing the EUS examination not to report code 76975 in conjunction with code 43259.

**43232** Esophagoscopy with transendoscopic ultrasound-guided intramural or transmural fine needle aspiration/biopsy(s).

**43238** EGD with transendoscopic ultrasound-guided intramural or transmural fine needle aspiration/biopsy(s) limited to the esophagus.

**43242** EGD with transendoscopic ultrasound-guided intramural or transmural fine needle aspiration/biopsy(s), which includes endoscopic ultrasound examination limited to the esophagus.
- Includes the diagnostic ultrasound supervision and interpretation (76975-26).
- Includes ultrasound guidance for biopsy (76942-26).

**43240** EGD with transmural drainage of pseudocyst.
- Indicates pancreatic pseudocyst.
- Ultrasound guidance can be billed if performed at time of drainage (76942-26).

**43219** Esophagoscopy with insertion of plastic tube or stent.

**43241** EGD with insertion of intraluminal tube or catheter placement.

**44370** Enteroscopy/small intestine endoscopy not including ileum with stent placement.

**44379** Enteroscopy/small intestine endoscopy including ileum with stent placement.
- Includes predilation.

**43245** EGD with dilation of gastric outlet.
- Does not include esophagus.
- If esophageal dilation is also performed at the same session, both 43249 and 43245 can be billed with the appropriate modifier.

**43257** EGD with delivery of thermal energy to the muscle of lower esophageal sphincter and/or gastric cardia, for treatment of gastroesophageal reflux disease (e.g., Stretta procedure).

### *Dilation Without Use of Endoscopy*

**43450** Dilation of the esophagus with unguided sound or bougie (Maloney, bougie dilatation), single or multiple passes.
- When performed with an endoscopy, the endoscopy can be separately billed because there are no combination codes that contain both the endoscopy and unguided dilation.

**43453** Dilation of the esophagus over guidewire.

**43456** Retrograde dilation of the esophagus by balloon or dilator.
- Can only be billed without the use of endoscopy.
- Retrograde means gaining entry below the esophagus, e.g., gastrostomy is utilized to insert bougie dilators.
- When radiologic guidance is used at the time of dilation, 74360-26 can also be billed when the documentation supports this.

**43458** Dilation of the esophagus with balloon (30 mm in diameter or larger) for achalasia.
- When performed with an endoscopy, the endoscopy can be separately billed because there are no combination codes that contain both the endoscopy and unguided dilation.
- Diagnosis code is only achalasia.
- The documentation in the endoscopy report must include the size of the balloon.

### *Tubes*

**43752** Naso/orogastric tube placement, requiring physician's skill and fluoroscopic guidance.
- This code includes fluoroscopic guidance, image documentation, and report.
- Usually performed in a hospital setting.

**43760** Change of gastrostomy tube.

- Includes removal and reinsertion of the gastrostomy tube.
- Can be performed at the office, at the bedside, or at an ASC.
- Separate codes for the removal of G-tubes without replacement do not exist. When the removal-only service is performed, it should be billed as an evaluation and management visit, as such service should be performed prior to the decision to remove the G-tube.

*NOTE: New codes were added in 2008 to report percutaneous tube placement (49440, 49441, and 49442) using radiological guidance. Code 43750 has been deleted, effective 2008. Code 43760 has been revised to clarify that it should be reported for tube conversion procedures that do not require imaging or endoscopic guidance. In addition, the cross-reference to code 75984 has been deleted.*

**43761** Repositioning of the gastric feeding tube, by any method, through the duodenum for enteric nutrition.

- The tube placement would be included in any endoscopic procedure.
- Can be billed with either nasogastric tube advancement or gastric tube advancement.
- If imaging guidance is performed, use code 75894.

**91100** Intestinal bleeding tube passage, positioning, and monitoring.

**91105** Gastric intubation and aspiration for lavage for treatment, such as ingested poisons.

**91000** Esophageal intubation and collection of washings for cytology, including preparation of specimens.

**91055** Gastric intubation, washings, and preparing slides for cytology

## B. Endoscopic Retrograde Cholangiopancreatography (ERCP)

**43260** Parent code; describes a diagnostic ERCP.

- The common bile duct is cannulated, dye is injected, and the pancreas and biliary tree are visualized.
- The collection of specimens by brushing or washing is included in reporting this code.
- If a surgical ERCP is performed during the same session, the diagnostic ERCP is not separately reported.
- If unable to inject either duct, modifier 53 should be amended to the claim indicating that it was a discontinued procedure.
- Radiologic supervision codes might be billable if radiologist does not participate in the interpretation of ERCP.
- If radiologic supervision and interpretation is performed at the time of the ERCP, codes 74328, 74329, or 74330, as appropriate, can be separately reported, if documented. Modifier 26 would be added to indicate interpretation, not ownership of equipment.

**43261** ERCP with biopsy.

- If radiologic supervision and interpretation is performed at the time of the dilation, codes 74328, 74329, or 74330 can be separately reported, if documented. Modifier 26 would be added to indicate interpretation, not ownership of equipment.

**43262** ERCP with sphincterotomy.

- The sphincter of Oddi is incised to allow the flow of bile.
- This code is also used for "papillotomy."

- If radiologic supervision and interpretation is performed at the time of the sphincterotomy, codes 74328, 74329, or 74330, as appropriate, can be separately reported, if documented. Modifier 26 would be added to indicate interpretation, not ownership of equipment.

**43263** ERCP with pressure measurement of the sphincter of Oddi in the pancreatic duct or common bile duct.

- If measurements are obtained from both the pancreatic and common bile ducts, the code can be reported twice by appending modifier 59 to the second procedure.
- If radiologic supervision and interpretation is performed at the time of the pressure measurement, codes 74328, 74329, or 74330, as appropriate, can be separately reported, if documented. Modifier 26 would be added to indicate interpretation, not ownership of equipment.

**43264** ERCP with removal of stone(s).

- Includes the balloon sweep to clear stones and debris from the duct.
- No minimum requirements on the size of stones.
- When performed with sphincterotomy, also use code 43262.
- If radiologic supervision and interpretation is performed at the time of the stone removal, codes 74328, 74329, or 74330, as appropriate, can be separately reported, if documented. Modifier 26 would be added to indicate interpretation, not ownership of equipment.

**43265** ERCP with destruction, lithotripsy of stones.

- Any method for destruction of stones can be used.
- When performed with sphincterotomy, also use code 43262.
- The removal of the stones is included and not separately billable unless performed at a separate session.
- If radiologic supervision and interpretation is performed at the time of the lithotripsy, codes 74328, 74329, or 74330, as appropriate, can be separately reported, if documented. Modifier 26 would be added to indicate interpretation, not ownership of equipment.

**43267** ERCP with insertion of nasobiliary or nasopancreatic drainage tube.

- If performed at the time of stent placement, only the stent placement is reportable.
- When performed with sphincterotomy, also use code 43262.
- If radiologic supervision and interpretation is performed at the time of the tube placement, codes 74328, 74329, or 74330, as appropriate, can be separately reported, if documented. Modifier 26 would be added to indicate interpretation, not ownership of equipment.

**43268** ERCP with insertion of tube or stent into bile or pancreatic duct.

- Only indicates one duct. If stents are placed into more than one duct, each procedure can be reported separately with modifier 59.
- When performed with sphincterotomy, also use code 43262.
- If radiologic supervision and interpretation is performed at the time of the stent placement, codes 74328, 74329, or 74330, as appropriate, can be separately reported, if documented.
- Cannot be billed with a tube or stent change. Modifier 26 would be added to indicate interpretation, not ownership of equipment.

**43269** ERCP with removal of foreign body and/or change of tube or stent.

- Only indicates one tube or stent. If more than one tube or stent is changed, each procedure can be reported with modifier 59.
- If radiologic supervision and interpretation is performed at the time of the foreign body or tube change/removal, codes 74328, 74329, or 74330, as appropriate, can be sepa-

rately reported, if documented. Modifier 26 would be added to indicate interpretation, not ownership of equipment.

**43271** Describes ERCP with balloon dilation of ampulla of Vater, biliary and/or pancreatic ducts.

- Includes more than one dilation.
- When performed with sphincterotomy, also use code 43262.
- If radiologic supervision and interpretation is performed at the time of the dilation, codes 74328, 74329, or 74330, as appropriate, can be separately reported, if documented. Modifier 26 would be added to indicate interpretation, not ownership of equipment.

**43272** ERCP with ablation of tumor(s), polyp(s), or other lesion(s) not amenable to removal by hot biopsy forceps, bipolar cautery, or snare technique.

- Includes more than one ablation.
- If radiologic supervision and interpretation is performed at the time of the ablation, codes 74328, 74329, or 74330, as appropriate, can be separately reported, if documented. Modifier 26 would be added to indicate interpretation, not ownership of equipment.

## C. Anoscopy, Proctosigmoidoscopy, Flexible Sigmoidoscopy, Colonoscopy, Colonoscopy Through Stoma, Ileoscopy, and Pouchoscopy

### *Definitions*

Anoscopy is the examination of the anus and distal rectum.
Proctosigmoidoscopy is the examination of the rectum and sigmoid colon.
Sigmoidoscopy is the examination of the entire rectum and sigmoid colon and may include examination of a portion of the descending colon.
Colonoscopy is the examination of the colon proximal to the splenic flexure.
Colonoscopy through stoma is the examination of the proximal colon through established abdominal wall stoma.
Ileoscopy is the examination of the ileum through established stoma into the small intestine.
Pouchoscopy is the examination of a small intestinal pouch through the anus or abdominal stoma into the small intestine.

- Codes for rigid proctosigmoidoscopy should be used when a proctoscope, a stiff hollow tube for examination of the rectum and sigmoid, is used.
- Codes for flexible sigmoidoscopy should be used when a flexible endoscope is used to examine the rectum and sigmoid.
- The flexible sigmoidoscope reaches substantially further than the rigid proctoscope.
- When a diagnostic colonoscopy is attempted and does not get past the splenic flexure, Medicare requires that a discontinued colonoscopy is billed with modifier 53. Commercial payers may have different requirements.

  *NOTE: According to CMS Program Memorandum (Transmittal AB-03-114), dated August 1, 2003, Medicare covers colorectal cancer screening test/procedures for the early detection of colorectal cancer when coverage conditions are met. Among the screening procedures covered are screening colonoscopies: G0105, Colorectal cancer screening; colonoscopy on individual at high risk; and G0121, Colorectal screening; colonoscopy on individual not meeting criteria for high risk. Coverage of these services is subject to certain frequency limitations.*
- In some instances, a provider may begin a screening colonoscopy, but, because of extenuating circumstances, be unable to complete the procedure. The incomplete screening

procedure should be billed with a 53 modifier. At a different time, the provider may attempt and complete the intended screening colonoscopy on the patient. This situation parallels those of diagnostic colonoscopies in which the provider is unable to complete the colonoscopy because of extenuating circumstances and must attempt a complete colonoscopy at a later time.

- If coverage conditions are met, Medicare pays for both the incomplete colonoscopy and the complete colonoscopy whether the colonoscopy is screening in nature or diagnostic.
- When the colonoscope is advanced beyond the splenic flexure but does not reach the cecum, commercial payers may require the use of modifier 52 for reduced service. For Medicare, an incomplete screening colonoscopy should be reported using modifier 53.
- Colonoscopy includes the examination of the terminal ileum; examination of the terminal ileum should not be separately reported with the use of the enteroscopy codes.
- Colonoscopy and flexible sigmoidoscopy may be done during the same session prior to colostomy reversal and would be separately reportable because they are performed through different entry points.
- Most Medicare contractors have Local Coverage Determinations governing colonoscopies. Please check with the Medicare contractor for your state because the policies vary from state to state.
- Tricare, the benefit program for active duty military, dependents, and retirees, has a coverage policy for screening and diagnostic colonoscopies that may differ from the Medicare contractor policy for your state.

**44380** Parent code; diagnostic ileoscopy. The endoscopist enters the ileum through an abdominal ileostomy stoma, not through the anus.

**44385** Parent code; diagnostic endoscopic evaluation of a small intestinal pouch (pouchoscopy). The endoscopist enters the pouch through the anus.

**43500** Parent code; diagnostic rigid proctosigmoidoscopy.

**43530** Parent code; diagnostic flexible sigmoidoscopy.

**43578** Parent code; diagnostic colonoscopy.

**44388** Parent code; diagnostic colonoscopy through stoma.

- When performed, collection of specimen(s) by brushing or washing is included in these codes.
- The codes are designated as a "separate procedure" and cannot be billed with any other code within the same family.

**45303** Proctosigmoidoscopy with dilation, any method.

**45340** Flexible sigmoidoscopy with dilation by balloon only, one or more strictures.

**45386** Colonoscopy with dilation by balloon only, one or more strictures.

**46604** Anoscopy with dilation, any method.

- Flexible sigmoidoscopy and colonoscopy dilation is by balloon only. Any other technique for dilation of the colon would be reported as an unlisted procedure.

**45337** Flexible sigmoidoscopy, with decompression of volvulus, any method.

**44382** Ileoscopy with biopsy. The endoscopist enters the ileum through an abdominal ileostomy stoma, not through the anus.

**44386** Pouchoscopy with biopsy. The endoscopist enters the pouch through the anus.

**44389** Colonoscopy through stoma with biopsy.

**45305** Proctosigmoidoscopy with biopsy.

**45331** Flexible sigmoidoscopy with biopsy.

**45380** Colonoscopy with biopsy.

**46606** Anoscopy with biopsy.

- This code is reported only one time regardless of whether single or multiple biopsies are performed.
- Code 45380, Colonoscopy, flexible, proximal to splenic flexure; with biopsy, single or multiple, does not describe a specific technique. The terminology is accepted and understood to mean the use of a forceps to grasp and remove a small piece of tissue without the application of cautery. Colonoscopy reports may describe the biopsy of a lesion or polyp using a cold forceps or may describe the biopsy without mentioning the specific device. The biopsy may be from an obvious lesion that is too large to remove, from a suspicious area of abnormal mucosa, or from a lesion or polyp so small that it can be completely removed during the performance of the biopsy, which is often demonstrated with the cold biopsy forceps technique. The service is reported with code 45380 regardless of the final histology of the piece of tissue obtained for analysis.
- The removal of a polyp using cold biopsy forceps is considered a biopsy and reported using the appropriate biopsy code for the procedure.

**44392** Colonoscopy through stoma with removal of tumor(s), polyp(s), or other lesion(s) by hot biopsy forceps or bipolar cautery.

**45308** Proctosigmoidoscopy with removal of tumor(s), polyp(s), or other lesion(s) by hot biopsy forceps or bipolar cautery.

**45339** Flexible sigmoidoscopy with removal of tumor(s), polyp(s), or other lesion(s) by hot biopsy forceps or bipolar cautery.

**45384** Colonoscopy with removal of tumor(s), polyp(s), or other lesion(s) by hot biopsy forceps or bipolar cautery.

**46612** Anoscopy with removal of tumor(s), polyp(s), or other lesion(s) by hot biopsy forceps, bipolar cautery or snare technique.

- Multiple lesions removed by hot biopsy are not reported separately.
- Different techniques performed at different sites within the intestine can be reported using the 59 modifier.
- When a colonoscopist documents the use of hot biopsy forceps to remove a lesion, code 45384, Colonoscopy, flexible, proximal to the splenic flexure; with removal of tumor(s), polyp(s), or other lesion(s) by hot biopsy forceps or bipolar cautery, is used to accurately report the service. Bipolar cautery and monopolar cautery forceps can be used to perform this service. Monopolar cautery forceps create heat in the metal portion of the forceps cup by causing current to flow from the device through the patient to a grounding pad. Bipolar cautery uses current that runs from one portion of the tip of the forceps device to another portion of the forceps device to heat the metal used to cauterize and remove a lesion or polyp. Again, remnants of the lesion after use of a cautery forceps can be cauterized or ablated to completely destroy the intended target.
- Anoscopy includes hot biopsy and snare in the description.

**44394** Colonoscopy through stoma with removal of tumor(s), polyp(s), or other lesion(s) by snare.

**45309** Proctosigmoidoscopy with removal of tumor(s), polyp(s), or other lesion(s) by snare.

**45338** Flexible sigmoidoscopy with removal of tumor(s), polyp(s), or other lesion(s) by snare.

**45385** Colonoscopy with removal of tumor(s), polyp(s), or other lesion(s) by snare.

- Multiple lesions removed by snare are not reported separately.
- Different techniques performed at different sites within the intestine can be reported using the 59 modifier.
- These codes can be used to report a cold or hot snare technique.
  - The snare technique is most often used to perform a polypectomy during a colonoscopy. When the snare cautery technique is employed, a wire loop is placed around the desired piece of tissue or polyp and is heated to shave off the lesion. Larger lesions may be removed with a single application of the snare or can be removed with several applications of the snare in pieces frequently described as "piecemeal." Remnants of the lesion after use of a snare can be cauterized or ablated to completely destroy the intended target but only one technique should be reported to remove a unique polyp or lesion.
  - Snare devices may also be used without electrocautery to "decapitate" small polyps. Most often the colonoscopy report will specify that a "snare technique" was used, but do not let alternative terminology confuse you. The report may also include the phrase "hot snare," "monopolar snare," "cold snare," or "bipolar snare," all of which should be reported using code 45385.

**44393** Colonoscopy through stoma with ablation of tumor(s), polyp(s), or other lesion(s) not amenable to removable by snare or hot biopsy.

**45315** Proctosigmoidoscopy with ablation of tumor(s), polyp(s), or other lesion(s) not amenable to removal by snare or hot biopsy.

**45339** Flexible sigmoidoscopy with ablation of tumor(s), polyp(s), or other lesion(s) not amenable to removable by snare or hot biopsy.

**45383** Colonoscopy with ablation of tumor(s), polyp(s), or other lesion(s) not amenable to removable by snare or hot biopsy.

**46615** Anoscopy with ablation of tumor(s), polyp(s), or other lesion(s) not amenable to removable by snare or hot biopsy.

- This code is reported only one time for any number of lesions removed by techniques other than snare or hot biopsy.
- The definition of 45383 can be misleading because it only states what techniques should not be used. It may not be possible to remove a lesion using another technique, and the lesion may or may not be biopsied before it is ablated using an alternative technique. In other cases, it may not be possible or necessary to obtain a tissue sample of a lesion or polyp depending on the location.
- Code 45383 is also frequently used to describe the treatment of benign vascular lesions, ablation of sessile polyps, arteriovenous malformations (AVMs), or other suspicious areas within the colon or anus.

- These codes can be used to describe procedures accomplished by argon plasma coagulation (APC), laser, or other methods.

**45335** Flexible sigmoidoscopy with directed submucosal injection(s), any substance.

**45381** Colonoscopy with directed submucosal injection(s), any substance.

- Includes the injection of medication such as Botox, India Ink (tattooing), saline, and/or steroids. It does not include injection of sclerosing solution. There are separate endoscopy codes for sclerosing solution.
- The procedure report may indicate that a polyp was injected with saline or "lifted" prior to removal by another technique. In other cases, injection will be performed to "tattoo" an area with India ink for later identification during a subsequent procedure or during surgery. In both of these cases, CPT code 45381, Colonoscopy, flexible, proximal to splenic flexure; with directed submucosal injection(s), any substance, should be reported as an additional service to any other therapeutic procedure.

**44397** Colonoscopy through stoma with stent placement.

**45327** Proctosigmoidoscopy with stent placement.

**45387** Colonoscopy with stent placement.

- Includes predilation.

**44391** Colonoscopy through stoma with control of bleeding.

**45334** Flexible sigmiodoscopy with control of bleeding.

**45382** Colonoscopy with control of bleeding.

**46614** Anoscopy with control of bleeding.

- Bleeding can be treated by several endoscopic techniques including, but not limited to, the following:
  - Application of cautery with heater probe, bipolar or monopolar probe.
  - Injection of vasocontrictive agents (e.g., epinephrine or irritant liquids).
  - Laser cautery.
- All methods used to control bleeding are reported using the one code.
- If bleeding occurs as a result of removal of a lesion by any method, control of bleeding is a component of the removal of the lesion and is not reported separately.
- If a lesion is identified in one region of the intestine, and a bleeding lesion in another part of the intestine is identified and controlled, different techniques performed at different sites within the intestine can be reported using the 59 modifier.

**45331** Flexible sigmoidoscopy with endoscopic ultrasound examination.

**45391** Colonoscopy with endoscopic ultrasound examination.

**45332** Flexible sigmoidoscopy with transendoscopic ultrasound-guided intramural or transmural fine needle aspiration/biopsy(s).

**45392** Colonoscopy with transendoscopic ultrasound-guided intramural or transmural fine needle aspiration/biopsy(s).

- Includes the diagnostic ultrasound supervision and interpretation (76975-26).
- Includes ultrasound guidance for biopsy (76942-26).

**96570** Photodynamic therapy by endoscopic application of light to ablate abnormal tissue via activation of photosensitive drug(s); first 30 minutes.

- Used in addition to endoscopy codes.
- Use code 96571 for each additional 15 minutes.

# VI. Medicare Payment Policy for Colorectal Cancer Screening

## A. Age and Frequency Limits for Colorectal Cancer Screenings

### *Fecal occult blood tests*

- Age 50 and over
- Once every 12 months

### *Flexible sigmoidoscopies*

- Age 50 and over
- Once every 48 months

### *Colonoscopies*

- Age 50 and over
- For high-risk individuals: once every 24 months
- For average-risk individuals: once every 10 years

### *Barium enemas*

- Age 50 and over
- For high-risk individuals: once every 24 months
- For average-risk individuals: once every 48 months

*NOTE: Under the Medicare regulations, colonoscopies, sigmoidoscopies, and barium enemas are not allowed in place of each other. If a patient had a sigmoidoscopy 24 months ago, they cannot have a screening barium enema for another 24 months, as the screening benefit for flexible sigmoidoscopies is once every 48 months.*

*NOTE: A high-risk person is one who has a family (first-degree relative) history of cancer, prior experience of cancer or precursor neoplastic polyps, a history of a chronic digestive disease condition such as inflammatory bowel disease, the presence of any appropriate recognized gene markers for colorectal cancer, or other predisposing factors.*

## B. Colorectal Cancer Screening G Codes

G codes, one type of Healthcare Common Procedure Coding System (HCPCS) code, are established by Medicare to address a programmatic need. Colorectal cancer screening services are covered under a specific benefit established by law. CMS has established codes and reimbursement for these services. These codes are used by Medicare contractors only, unless instructed to do so by a commercial insurance carrier. If the patient has symptoms and/or is referred for a colonoscopy based on abnormal laboratory and/or physical findings, the service or surgery codes are reported in place of the screening G codes.

*NOTE: Medicare does not pay for services in the absence of signs or symptoms, unless specifically provided by law. The visit preceding a screening colonoscopy for a patient without signs or symptoms is not billable. Do not use an advance beneficiary notice (ABN).*

**G0104** Colorectal cancer screening; flexible sigmoidoscopy.

- Is used for screening flexible sigmoidoscopy.
- Is covered at a frequency of once every 48 months for patients over 50.
- If during the course of the screening flexible sigmoidoscopy a lesion or a growth is detected that results in a biopsy or removal of the growth, the appropriate category I code (active, billable codes for which there is a relative value assigned) to describe flexible sigmoidoscopy with biopsy removal, polypectomy, or ablation of the lesion should be used instead of G0104.
- If the patient has had a screening colonoscopy (code G0121) within the past 10 years (at least 119 months between the last screening colonoscopy), then G0104 would be denied by Medicare as "not medically necessary."

**G0105** Colorectal cancer screening; high-risk individual.

- To be used for screening colonoscopy for an individual at high risk.
- Is covered at a frequency of once every 24 months (at least 23 months from the last screening colonoscopy) for those at high risk of colon cancer.
- If during the course of the screening colonoscopy a lesion or growth is detected that results in a biopsy or removal of the growth, then the appropriate category I code to describe a colonoscopy with biopsy, removal, polypectomy, or ablation of the lesion should be billed instead of screening colonoscopy.

**82270** Colorectal cancer screening; consecutive collected specimens with single determination.

- Is used for colorectal cancer screening using fecal-occult blood tests.
- Is covered at a frequency of once every 12 months for anyone over age 50.
- Is paid under clinical laboratory fee schedule.

**G0394** Blood occult test (e.g., guaiac), feces, for single determination for colorectal neoplasm (e.g., patient was provided three cards or one triple card for consecutive collection).

- Even though it is a G code, this code is not for screening but for actual symptoms because 82270 became a screening code for Medicare in 2007.
- There is a National Coverage Decision Policy that includes everything other than screening.

**G0106** Colorectal cancer screening; barium enema (alternative to G0104).

*NOTE: Code G0107 has been deleted and was replaced with code 82270.*

**G0120** Colorectal cancer screening; barium enema (alternative to G0105).

- G0106 and G0120 are used for a barium enema for colorectal cancer screening when the barium enema is substituted for either the sigmoidoscopy or colonoscopy procedure.

**G0121** Colorectal cancer screening colonoscopy on individual not meeting criteria for high risk.

- G0121 is used when the individual does not meet the criteria for high risk for colon cancer.
- Is covered at a frequency of once every 10 years.
- If during the course of the screening colonoscopy a lesion or growth is detected that results in a biopsy or removal of the growth, then the appropriate category I code to describe a colonoscopy with biopsy, removal, polypectomy, or ablation of the lesion should be billed instead of screening colonoscopy.

**G0122** Colorectal cancer screening; barium enema.

- G0122 is used when the individual does not meet the criteria for high risk.

*NOTE: Effective January 1, 2007, CMS waives the annual Part B deductible for colorectal cancer screening tests. Unfortunately, if the screening procedure turns in to a therapeutic procedure, such as a biopsy or removal of a lesion, CMS has stated that the procedure cannot be coded as a screening and the deductible is no longer waived.*

**CMS advises that, whether or not an abnormality is found, if a service to a Medicare beneficiary starts out as a screening examination (colonoscopy or sigmoidoscopy), then the primary diagnosis should be the appropriate screening code. The secondary diagnosis code should be the ICD-9-CM code for the abnormal finding (polyp, etc.). The appropriate CPT code to use is the procedure actually performed, not a screening G code. Enter a "2" in Box 24E of the CMS 1500 to link the biopsy or polypectomy with the polyp.**

# VII. Multiple Endoscopy Policy

The multiple endoscopy policy for Medicare went into effect on April 1, 1993. As of the date of the publication of this manual, this policy is still in effect. The policy found in Medicare Carriers Manual, section 15038 states:

Multiple Endoscopies: For multiple endoscopic procedures, use the full value of the highest valued endoscopy plus the difference between the next highest and the base endoscopy (the parent code). For example, in the course of performing a fiberoptic colonoscopy (code 45378), a physician performs a biopsy (code 45380) and removes a polyp (code 45385). Both codes 45380 and 45385 contain the values of the base endoscopy, code 45378. Use the actual value of code 45385 plus the difference between 45380 and 45378. The endoscopic base codes are listed in the Medicare Fee Schedule Data Base (MFSDB). For further information, see §4826.C.12.

# VIII. Other Biopsies or Treatments

## A. Anorectal Biopsy

**45100** Biopsy of the anorectal wall, anal approach.

- Can also be performed as a suction biopsy.
- Can be performed by pediatric gastroenterologist or colorectal surgeon to diagnose Hirschsprung's disease or congenital megacolon.
- Has a 90-day global surgery package.
- If more tissue has to be obtained in a subsequent procedure during the global period, modifier 58 would be attached to the repeat biopsy procedure performed during the 90-day global period.

## B. Liver Biopsy

**47000** Biopsy of the liver by percutaneous needle.

- If performed with ultrasound guidance, 76942-26 can be reported separately.
- If performed with computed tomography guidance, 76360-26 can be reported separately.
- If performed with magnetic resonance guidance, 76393-26 can be reported separately.
- If performed with fluoroscopic guidance, 77003-26 can be reported separately.
- If multiple radiological guidance are performed, for example where both ultrasound and fluoroscopic guidance are used, only one technique can be reported.

### C. Hemorrhoid Treatments

**46221** Hemorrhoidectomy, by simple ligature, e.g., rubber band

**46934** Destruction of hemorrhoids, any method; internal

### D. Paracentesis

**49080** Paritoneocentesis, abdominal paracentesis, or peritoneal lavage (diagnostic or therapeutic); initial

**49081** Subsequent

## IX. Diagnostic Tests

### A. Esophageal Studies

**91010** Esophageal motility study.

**91011** Esophageal motility study with a stimulant such as mecholyl.

**91012** Esophageal motility study with acid perfusion studies.

- Only the most extensive procedure can be reported.
- Involves inserting a probe/sensor into the esophagus for esophageal motility studies.
- If performed in an independent diagnostic testing facility, outpatient, or inpatient hospital setting, modifier 26 would be added to the procedure to describe the physician interpretation.

**91034** Esophagus, gastroesophageal reflux test with nasal catheter pH electrode(s) placement, recording, analysis, and interpretation.

- A small, thin probe, or electrode, that measures the pH (acidity) level within the esophagus is affixed at the end of flexible nasal catheter tubing. The catheter is inserted through the nose down to the target area in the esophagus, usually determined by manometry, and then connected to a data recorder. The probe records the pH level within the esophagus.

**91035** Esophagus, gastroesophageal reflux test with mucosal attached telemetry pH electrode placement, recording, analysis, and interpretation (Bravo).

- A small capsule containing a radiotelemetry pH sensor is inserted endoscopically in the esophagus and temporarily attached to the esophageal wall. The capsule monitors esophageal pH levels over a prolonged testing period. This information is transmitted to an external pager-sized receiver worn by the patient that records pH levels. After the prolonged testing period, the data are downloaded from the receiver to a computer that contains software for analyzing pH levels. The capsule does not need to be removed as it spontaneously detaches within 7 to 10 days and passes through the digestive tract.
- When billing for the professional component, the date of service is the date that the data are downloaded for analysis.

**91037** Esophageal function test, gastroesophageal reflux test with nasal catheter intraluminal impedance electrode(s) placement, recording, analysis, and interpretation.

**91038** Esophageal function test, gastroesophageal reflux test with nasal catheter intraluminal impedance electrode(s) placement, recording, analysis and interpretation; prolonged (greater than 1 hour, up to 24 hours).

- An impedance probe affixed to flexible nasal catheter tubing is inserted through the nose down to the lower esophageal sphincter following location of the lower sphincter by manometry. The patient is then given a liquid or solid bolus to swallow. As the bolus passes through the esophagus, the average electrical resistance between two adjacent electrodes (impedance) is then measured. The electrodes detect esophageal contraction and expansion and movement of the bolus through the esophagus in real time, as well as any gastroesophageal reflux. Esophageal function is evaluated by calculating the bolus transport time (BTT), which is the time it takes the bolus to pass from the proximal measuring segment and exit through the distal measuring segment. Contraction wave velocity (CWV), which is the speed of the contraction wave from the proximal measuring segment to the distal measuring segment, is also evaluated. This test is also referred to as multichannel intraluminal impedance testing or MII. Report 91037 for a recording of 1 hour or less. Report 91038 for prolonged or ambulatory recording of greater than 1 hour, up to 24 hours.

When billing for 91038, the date the study was acquired for analysis is the date of the procedure.

- If performed in an independent diagnostic testing facility or an outpatient or inpatient hospital setting, modifier 26 would be added to the procedure to indicate physician interpretation.
- To report the performance of esophageal function and motility studies, report both procedures.
- To report the performance of esophageal function and esophageal pH studies, report both procedures.

**91040** Esophageal balloon distension provocation study. Evaluates chest pain suspected to be noncardiac in origin.

**91000** Esophageal intubation and collection of washings for cytology.

**91055** Gastric intubation, washings, and preparing slides for cytology.

## B. Upper Gastrointestinal Diagnostic Tests

**91020** Gastric motility (manometric) studies.

**91022** Duodenal motility (manometric) studies.

- To report studies involving both the esophagus and the stomach, report only the most comprehensive service (i.e., the gastric motility [manometric] study).
- To report studies involving both the stomach and the duodenum, report both the services.
- If fluoroscopy is performed to position the duodenal motility catheter, report 76000.

**91132** Electrogastrography, diagnostic, transcutaneous.

**91133** Electrogastrography, transcutaneous, with provocative testing.

**91065** Breath hydrogen test (e.g., for detection of lactase deficiency), fructose intolerance, bacterial overgrowth, or oro-cecal gastrointestinal transit).

**78268** *Helicobacter pylori* breath test analysis, using the C-14 radioactive isotope.

**83013** *Helicobacter pylori* breath test analysis for urease activity, using the C-13 nonradioactive isotope.

**87338** *Helicobacter pylori,* stool analysis.

**87339** *Helicobacter pylori,* enzyme immunoassay analysis.

**83009** *Helicobacter pylori,* blood test analysis, for urease activity, using the C-13 nonradioactive isotope.

## C. Capsule Endoscopy

**91110** GI tract imaging, intraluminal, of the esophagus through ileum (wireless capsule endoscopy).

- As of April 2007, endoscopic placement of the capsule can be separately reported using the appropriate code of the endoscopic technique. However, because part of the upper GI tract has already been visualized during the endoscopic placement, modifier 52 should be added (e.g., 91110-52 if done in office as place of service or 91110-26-52 if done other than office setting).
- Only covered if previous upper GI endoscopy and colonoscopy were negative. Some carriers may also require a negative small bowel follow through.
- Still not covered by some payers.
- If the ileum is not visualized, modifier 52 should be added.

**91111** GI tract imaging, intraluminal (e.g., capsule endoscopy), esophagus with physician interpretation and report.

- The significant difference between codes 91110 and 91111 is in the physician work portion of the service as it relates to the review and interpretation of the generated images and creating the report. Capsule endoscopy studies of the esophagus, code 91111, involve physician examination of video images limited to the esophagus. Code 91110 includes video images from the esophagus to the ileum.
- Only approved for diagnosis code of portal hypertension; requires a secondary diagnosis of varices by CMS.

## D. Anorectal Diagnostic Tests

**91122** Anorectal manometry.

**91120** Rectal sensation, tone, and compliance test (i.e., response to graded balloon distension).

- For biofeedback training, use code 90911.

## E. Paracentesis

**49080** Abdominal paracentesis, or peritoneal lavage (diagnostic or therapeutic); initial.

**49081** Abdominal paracentesis, or peritoneal lavage (diagnostic or therapeutic); subsequent.

- The physician withdraws fluid from the abdominal cavity (paracentesis) or performs infusion and drainage of fluid from the abdominal cavity (peritoneal lavage). The

| Code | Descriptor | Add-on Code |
|---|---|---|
| 90760 | Intravenous infusion, hydration; initial, up to one (1) hour | |
| 90761 | Intravenous infusion, hydration; each additional hour, up to eight (8) hours (list separately in addition to code for primary procedure) | Yes |
| 90765 | Intravenous infusion, for therapy/diagnosis (specify substance or drug); initial, up to one (1) hour | |
| 90766 | Intravenous infusion, for therapy/diagnosis (specify substance of drug); each additional hour, up to eight (8) hours (list separately in addition to code for primary procedure) | Yes |
| 90767 | Intravenous infusion, for therapy/diagnosis (specify substance or drug); addition sequential infusion, up to one (1) hour (list separately in addition to code for primary procedure) | Yes |
| 90768 | Intravenous infusion, for therapy/diagnosis (specify substance or drug); concurrent infusion (list separately in addition to code for primary procedure) | Yes |
| 90772 | Therapeutic or diagnostic injection (specify substance or drug); subcutaneous or intramuscular | |
| 90774 | Therapeutic or diagnostic injection (specify substance or drug); intravenous push, single or initial substance/drug | |
| 90775 | Therapeutic or diagnostic injection (specify substance or drug); each additional sequential intravenous push (list separately in addition to code for primary procedure) | Yes |
| 96401 | Chemotherapy administration, subcutaneous or intramuscular; nonhormonal antineoplastic | |

physician inserts a needle or catheter into the abdominal cavity and withdraws and drains fluid for diagnostic or therapeutic purposes. The needle or catheter is removed at the completion of the procedure. In 49081, this is done subsequent to a previous peritoneocentesis procedure.

**49420** Insertion of intraperitoneal cannula or catheter for drainage or dialysis; temporary.

- The physician places a temporary intraperitoneal catheter for drainage or dialysis. The physician makes a small abdominal incision and inserts the catheter into the cavity. The proximal end of the catheter is tunneled subcutaneously away from the initial incision and brought out through the skin.

## F. Infusion Therapies

Agents such as infliximab, natalizumab, and porfimer sodium are administered through infusion therapy. In order to bill for the infusion of these drugs in the physician office, the physician/provider has to be in the office suite when the service is provided.

An ambulatory surgical center (ASC) is not a Medicare-approved site for infusion therapy.

Effective January 1, 2006, CPT revised the coding for infusion services. Monoclonal antibodies such as infliximab and natalizumab, as well as porfimer sodium for photodynamic therapy, can be billed using the chemotherapy codes.

The codes used for infliximab or natalizumab infusion are:

**96413** Chemotherapy administration, intravenous infusion technique: up to 1 hour single or initial substance/drug.

**96415** Each additional hour, 1 to 8 hours (list separately in addition to code for primary procedure). Partial hour infusions must be 31 minutes or greater to qualify for another unit of 96415.

In addition to the infusion code, bill the injectible using J1745, Injection, infliximab, 10 mg; J2323, Injection, natalizumab, 1 mg; or J9600, Injection, porfimer sodium, 75mg.

Some Medicare contractors have issued a Local Coverage Determination concerning infliximab or natalizumab therapy. The most common ICD-9-CM codes to support the infusion in gastroenterology are:

| | |
|---|---|
| 555.0–555.9 | Regional enteritis |
| 556.0–556.9 | Ulcerative colitis |
| 565.1 | Anal fistula |
| 569.81 | Fistula of intestine, excluding rectum and anus |

The medication must be obtained, administered, and billed by the physician. The receipt (proof of purchase) must be kept on file to validate billing for medications.

### G. Colorectal Screening by CT Colonography

Until recently CT colonography was not recognized as a recommended screening option for colorectal cancer. When billing for CT colonography, unless otherwise specified by your local carriers or payers, you must use one of the two category III CPT tracking codes:

**0066T** Computed tomographic (CT) colonography (i.e., virtual colonoscopy); screening.

**0067T** Computed tomographic (CT) colonography (i.e., virtual colonoscopy); diagnostic.

CPT category III tracking codes are a set of temporary codes used to identify and track emerging technology, services, and procedures. These codes allow data collection for these services/procedures to determine clinical efficacy, utilization, and outcomes.

## X. Coding an Unlisted Procedure

Although there are thousands of CPT codes, there may not be a code that accurately defines the procedure that was performed. This can be the case for a new device or technique, as it can take several years from the time a new device is available until a code is submitted to the CPT Editorial Panel for consideration. Even if the Panel approves a code, it can be several years before a new code appears. There are also situations where a procedure is performed so infrequently that it does not meet the criteria to warrant establishing a separate code. In either case, there are ways to get paid for a procedure for which there is no code.

If the procedure is an add-on to an existing code, such as insertion of a decompression tube during a colonoscopy, there are two options available for obtaining payment for the physician work of this portion of the procedure: *1*) bill the colonoscopy with a 22 modifier indicating the procedure involved more work than is defined by the code, or 2) code the colonoscopy together with an unlisted procedure code.

Unlisted codes end with 99 and are at the end of each section of CPT. When an unlisted procedure code is used, or if the procedure is billed with a 22 modifier, documentation including operative/procedure reports should be provided to the carrier. Medical journal articles, general descriptions of the service, and "special reports" are examples of other supporting documentation that may be provided. A special report should include the following:

- Definition or description of the nature, extent, and need for the procedure.
- The time, effort, and equipment necessary to provide the service.
- The complexity of symptoms, final diagnosis, and pertinent physical findings.
- Diagnostic and therapeutic procedures.
- Concurrent problems.
- Extent of follow-up care required.

The special report or cover letter should also identify procedures for which there is a code and reimbursement that are similar to the unlisted procedure in terms of work effort, time, and expense.

Because any procedure that is submitted with an unlisted procedure code will have to be manually reviewed and priced, payment will take significantly longer than for services for which there is a category I code and a published fee. Often the payment will be dependent on the reviewer and may vary each time the procedure is submitted.

chapter 1

# Review Questions

## Gastroenterology Coding Principles

***Identify the letter of the choice that best completes the statement or answers the question.***

1. A 54-year-old male was seen by Dr. Hyde in consultation for Dr. Jekyll with an abnormal upper GI series indicating a mass in the antrum of the stomach. He has COPD, history of MI with symptoms of angina, and a personal history of prostate cancer and is on prednisone for the COPD. The patient had a detailed history and comprehensive exam. The patient was scheduled for an upper GI endoscopy. Which of the following CPT codes describes the encounter?
   a. 99243 Office consultation for a new or established patient, which requires these three key components: a detailed history, a detailed examination, and medical decision making of low complexity. Counseling and/or coordination of care with other providers or agencies are provided consistent with the nature of the problem(s) and the patient's and/or family's needs. Usually, the presenting problem(s) are of moderate severity.
   b. 99242 Office consultation for a new or established patient, which requires these three key components: an expanded problem-focused history, an expanded problem-focused examination, and straightforward medical decision making. Counseling and/or coordination of care with other providers or agencies are provided consistent with the nature of the problem(s) and the patient's and/or family's needs. Usually, the presenting problem(s) are of low severity.
   c. 99203 Office or other outpatient visit for the evaluation and management of a new patient, which requires these three key components: a detailed history, a detailed examination, and medical decision making of low complexity. Counseling and/or coordination of care with other providers or agencies are provided consistent with the nature of the problem(s) and the patient's and/or family's needs. Usually, the presenting problem(s) are of moderate severity.
   d. 99244 Office consultation for a new or established patient, which requires these three key components: a comprehensive history, a comprehensive examination, and medical decision making of moderate complexity. Counseling and/or coordination of care with other providers or agencies are provided consistent with the nature of the problem(s) and the patient's and/or family's needs. Usually, the presenting problem(s) are of moderate to high severity.

2. The correct diagnosis code(s) to assign for the visit would be:
   a. 793.4
   b. 239.0, 496, 414.8, V58.65
   c. 789.36, 496, 414.8
   d. 793.4, 496, 414.8, V58.65

3. Modifier 59 is used when the following circumstances occur:
   a. Distinct service performed at separate site, separate procedure, and/or separate session.
   b. Multiple medical procedures performed at the same session by the same provider.
   c. When a separate procedure designation is made on one of the codes reported and you want to receive reimbursement for both services.
   d. A combination of medical and operative procedures performed at the same session by the same provider.

4. An esophageal dilation by balloon is attempted (43456) but fails. An endoscopic esophageal dilation is immediately performed (43220) and is successful. Code this encounter as:
   a. 43220 and 43456-52
   b. 43220 and 43456-51
   c. 43220
   d. 43456

5. An esophagoscopy with removal of lesions is conducted using hot biopsy forceps for three lesions and the snare technique for six lesions. The procedures would be reported as:
   a. 43216-76; 43217-51
   b. 43217; 43216-59
   c. 43228
   d. 43216-51; 43217-51

6. An esophagoscopy with dilation of the esophagus using a balloon of 36 mm with radiologic guidance in the treatment of achalasia would be coded as:
   a. 43320; 74360-51
   b. 43320-51
   c. 43458-51
   d. 43200; 43458; 74360-26

7. A simple surgical procedure with a rigid instrument to examine the rectum and distal colon that included dilation would be coded as:
   a. 43500-59
   b. 45303
   c. 45330
   d. 45338

8. During the course of a screening colonoscopy of a high-risk individual, a polyp was seen and removed using hot biopsy forceps. The procedure would be coded as:
   a. 45384
   b. G0104
   c. G0105-22
   d. 45378

9. What is true about HCPCS code G0121, Colorectal cancer screening colonoscopy on an individual not meeting the criteria for high risk?
   a. Is indicated for patients with a family history of colon cancer.
   b. Is allowed every 5 years.

c. Diagnosis code of V76.51 should be assigned.
d. Can only be billed to Medicare.

10. When bleeding results from an endoscopic service, the control of the bleeding at the time of service is:
    a. A separately reportable procedure using modifier 22.
    b. A separately reportable procedure using modifier 52.
    c. Included in the endoscopic procedure but reported as an add-on code.
    d. Included in the endoscopic procedure and is not coded separately.

chapter 2

# Medical Record Documentation

Documentation is the recording of pertinent facts and observations about an individual's health history, including past and present illnesses, tests, treatments, and outcomes.

The medical record chronologically documents the care of the patient in order to:

- Enable the physician and other health care professionals to plan and evaluate the patient's treatment.
- Enhance communication and promote continuity of care among physicians and other health care professionals involved in the patient's care.
- Facilitate claims review and payment.
- Assist in utilization review and quality of care evaluations.
- Reduce problems related to medical review.
- Provide clinical data for research and education.
- Serve as a legal document to verify care provided (e.g., in defense of an alleged professional liability claim).

## I. General Concepts

### A. What Payers Want and Why

Payers want to know that they are getting value for their health care dollars.

They may request additional documentation to validate that services provided were:

- Appropriate to treatment of the patient's condition
- Medically necessary for the diagnosis and/or treatment of an illness or injury
- Coded correctly

## B. Medically Necessary Services

Medically necessary services are those services or supplies that are:

- In accordance with standards of good medical practice
- Consistent with the diagnosis
- The most appropriate level of care provided in the most appropriate setting

## C. The Importance of Documentation and Coding

With clear information from the provider as documented, the coder can choose accurate and specific diagnosis and procedure codes. Specific codes have the best potential reimbursement value.

Failure to be aware of the rules or failure to understand them is no excuse in post-payment reviews. Office staff is expected to know the rules and adhere to them.

Good documentation is the only defense in the case of audits and post-payment reviews.

"If it wasn't documented, it wasn't done." This is the coder's motto. If the medical record shows no evidence of the performance of a test, procedure, or service, the reimbursement for the same must be returned and an overpayment interest penalty paid.

If fraud or abuse is suspected, a $2,000 per line item penalty could be assessed. Overutilization, overcharging and suspect billing practices can cause audits, too. In addition, tips from patients, employees, or even other physician offices can lead to a review or audit.

The best course for any coder is to stay informed. The coder should read coding materials, attend seminars and workshops, subscribe to newsletters and electronic newsgroups, attend meetings, and analyze explanation of benefits. Above all, the coder should monitor claims carefully.

# II. Principles of Documentation

## A. Basic Requirements

Documentation is the recording of pertinent facts and observations about an individual's health history, including past and present illnesses, tests, treatment, and outcomes. Documentation promotes communication between health care providers and payers.

1. **The medical record should be complete and legible.**
2. The documentation of each patient encounter should include:
    - Date of service
    - Reason for the encounter (subjective symptoms)
    - Appropriate history and physical exam (objective symptoms)
    - Review of lab, X-ray data, and other ancillary services
    - Assessment of the patient's condition
    - Plan of care (including discharge plan, if appropriate)
3. Past as well as present diagnoses should be available to the treating and/or consulting physician.
4. The reason for and results of X-rays, lab tests, and other ancillary services should be documented or included in the medical record.
5. Relevant health risk factors should be identified.
6. The patient's progress, including response to treatment, change in treatment, change in diagnosis, and patient's noncompliance, should be documented.

7. The written plan of care should include, when appropriate:
   - Treatments and medications specifying frequency and dosage
   - Any referrals and consultations
   - Patient/family education
   - Specific instructions for follow-up
8. The documentation should support the intensity of the patient evaluation and/or the treatment, including thought processes and the complexity of medical decision making.
9. The CPT/ICD-9-CM codes reported on the health insurance claim form or billing statement should reflect the documentation in the medical record.

## B. Style and Format

The SOAP format is the most popular for its simplicity. The format allows for the statement of Subjective and Objective factors as well as the physician's Assessment and the Plan for the patient's care and follow-up.

**SOAP Format**

| | |
|---|---|
| **S** | Subjective complaints, presenting problems, etc. |
| **O** | Objective factors, observable findings |
| **A** | Assessment, diagnostic process, probable diagnosis(es), total impression based on subjective and objective factors |
| **P** | Plan for treatment to include medications, tests, return visit information, medication side effects, instructions for notifying office, etc. |

The CHEDDAR format takes SOAP even further. It includes the Chief complaint, History, Exam, Details, Diagnosis(es), Assessment (plan for), and Return.

**CHEDDAR Format**

| | |
|---|---|
| **C** | Chief complaint: presenting problem, subjective statements |
| **H** | History: social, family, and physical history of presenting problem as well as contributing information |
| **E** | Examination, including extent of body system(s) examined |
| **D** | Details of problem and complaints, etc. |
| **D** | Drugs and dosage: a list of current medications used with dosage and frequency, etc. |
| **A** | Assessment of observations, etc.: Adding all known factors into either possible or defined diagnosis(es) as well as orders for diagnostic testing, lab testing, etc., medication changes and warnings regarding side effects, etc. |
| **R** | Return visit information, if applicable |

The Documentation Guidelines for the Evaluation and Management Services issued jointly in 1995 and 1997 by the American Medical Association (AMA) and the Health Care Financing Agency (HCFA), now the Centers for Medicare and Medicaid Services (CMS), incorporate the CHEDDAR methodology for documentation.

## III. Characteristics of Good Documentation

Good documentation is the start of correct coding. The following characteristics should be reviewed before coding:

1. Legibility
2. Completeness
   - Does the information flow logically?
   - Are there any information gaps?
   - Are there abnormal test results without explanatory documentation?
   - Is there conflicting documentation in the patient record?
   - Are there any required reports that are missing?
3. Timeliness, prescribed by regulations and law. Don't code without documentation.
4. Authentication. Is the physician's signature on the documentation?

## IV. Corrections and Alterations

Because of human error, it is inevitable that mistakes will be made. They should be corrected in the following manner when they do occur:

1. Put a line through the documentation made in error. The line should allow the documentation to show through; don't smear it out or cross it out completely.
2. Write the word "error" above the line.
3. Initial and date just after the word error.
4. Never use erasures, correction fluid, or other "cover-up" techniques to change records.
5. Make the corrections or additions and initial and date them as well.

Practices using electronic medical record (EMR) systems should consult with their EMR vendor for information on how to make corrections to EMRs.

## V. Assumption Coding and Physician Query Process

Assumption coding is assuming from clinical evidence on the patient's record that the patient has a specific diagnosis. This is prohibited.

Coders can avoid assumption coding by checking with the physician using the following guidelines:

1. Ask only questions that are drawn from the clinical documentation.
2. Ask only open-ended questions, if possible. If not, provide reasonable choices for the physician, so it does not appear that you are showing preference for a particular response.
3. Never make any clinical assumptions.
4. Remember that your role in the coding function is to translate the physician's documentation into billable "coding" language.
5. It is appropriate to ask for clarification, but maintain a strict and literal interpretation of the documentation as possible.

chapter 2

# Review Questions

## Medical Record Documentation

***Indicate whether the sentence or statement is true or false.***

T F 1. "If it wasn't documented, it wasn't done" is the coder's motto.

T F 2. The written plan of care does not have to be included in a progress note.

T F 3. The documentation does not have to support the CPT and ICD-9-CM codes that are billed.

T F 4. Assumption coding occurs when the coder codes a patient's condition because the physician did not document the level of detail needed to code a diagnosis.

T F 5. The documentation must support the medical necessity of the codes billed.

T F 6. To change a mistake made in medical documentation you may erase the mistake or use correction fluid and write over the mistake.

***Complete each sentence or statement.***

7. Two types of documentation formats are ____________________ and ____________________.

8. Medical documentation serves as a ____________________ to verify care provided.

9. Two reasons a payer may request additional documentation to validate the services provided are ____________________ and ____________________.

chapter 3

# Coding and the CPT Manual

## I. Basics Review

### A. What Is Coding?

- Procedure coding, CPT: relates "what" was done
- Diagnostic coding, ICD-9-CM: relates "why" it was done

### B. Why Is It Important to Code Properly?

- Maximize reimbursement to the provider rendering the service.
- Efficiency in the office: It is better to receive a check than a denied or pended claim.
- Coding is the process by which physicians are reimbursed, and coding protects against fraud and abuse.

### C. Observations About CPT

- CPT codes describe procedures and other professional services rendered in:
    - Office or other outpatient settings
    - Hospitals
    - Nursing facilities, domiciliaries, rest homes, patient's home, and custodial care centers
- The task of the coder is to find the code(s) with the highest degree of accuracy that best describes the procedure(s) performed.
- The CPT code chosen should reflect an accurate description of the exact service rendered.
- Coding requires extensive knowledge and familiarity with:
    - Medical terminology
    - Anatomy
    - Physiology
- Each procedure, service, or supply has a 5-digit numerical code. A number system is used to simplify the reimbursement process for insurance carriers, eliminating the need to read lengthy reports describing services.

- The 5-digit numbers can be modified by adding a 2-digit number to give additional information about the service.
- Sections are set up anatomically. The human body is segmented in order: outside to inside, top to bottom, front to back.
- Each code describes something different. Codes can change each year. Outdated codes do not get reimbursed.
- The CPT manual is divided into the following major sections:
  - Introduction
  - Evaluation and Management (E/M)
  - Anesthesia
  - Surgery
  - Radiology
  - Pathology and Laboratory
  - Medicine
- Currently, there are 13 appendixes to the CPT manual that cover the following topics:
  - Modifiers
  - Additions, Deletions, and Revisions
  - Clinical Examples
  - Add-on Codes
  - Codes Exempt from the 51 Modifier
  - Codes Exempt from the 63 Modifier
  - Codes that Include Moderate (Conscious) Sedation
  - Alphabetical Index of Performance Measures by Clinical Condition or Topic
  - Genetic Testing Code Modifiers
  - Electrodiagnostic Medicine Listing of Sensory, Motor, and Mixed Nerves
  - Product Pending FDA Approval
  - Vascular Families
  - Crosswalk to Deleted CPT Codes
- Each major section has its own set of rules, notes, and instructions. Coders must read them in order to code properly. Shortcuts frequently shorten reimbursement.
- CPT is revised annually in October and is effective January 1. There is no longer a grace period for using the new codes. Coders need to order a new CPT manual annually. There are typically hundreds of changes each year.

## II. Conventions for Locating CPT Codes

- Alphabetic index of procedures, organs, and conditions is in the back of the book.
- Bold-faced main terms may be followed by descriptions and groups of indented terms.
- A circle (●) in front of a code indicates a new code.
- A triangle (▲) indicates a new or revised description.
- A plus (+) in front of a code indicates that it is an add-on code and must be billed with another code in that family of codes.
- Some code descriptions are indented to show that they include the initial phrase from the nonindented code above, which is known as the "parent" code.
- The words in the description of the parent code that precede the semicolon are common to all the indented codes below.

# III. Proper Coding with CPT

- Identify the procedures, tests, services, equipment, supplies, etc., from the source document (i.e., superbill, medical record). Look for any modifying or extenuating circumstances.
- Identify main terms and subterms.
- Locate the procedure or service in the index by checking procedure name, anatomic site, synonym, eponym, and abbreviated entries, as necessary.
- When you have found the procedure, service, or alpha wording desired in the index, identify the code number next to it and refer to that code section in the basic manual. Be sure they match.
- If a range of codes is given for the procedure, read the description of each entry within the range to make the proper selection that matches or fits as closely as possible to what was actually done.
- Remember to never code directly from the index. Always use codes from the main body of the CPT manual.
- Ensure you have followed all notes and guidelines at the beginning of the section.
- If the exact code is not what you are looking for, you may want to use a modifier such as 22 or 52.
- If there is not a proper code, you may have to utilize "unlisted procedure" codes in that section. Only use them as a last resort. Do not do creative coding.
- Write the code number on the CMS1500 form or enter the code into the computer. Check and recheck that you have the proper code and have not transposed any digits. With no description allowed in the CMS1500, errors in the code can mean denial.
- Ensure that what you have coded (and therefore "charged") is documented in the medical record. If it isn't documented, it wasn't performed.
- Inclusion or exclusion of a code in CPT does not guarantee reimbursement by third-party payers.
- Incorrect coding leads to incorrect reimbursement, and possible "flagging" for audits or fraud and abuse for which there are heavy penalties.
- Make sure the diagnosis justifies the procedure.
- Ensure that all information needed on the insurance form or computer program is filled out for proper reimbursement.

# IV. Unlisted Procedures

- Each section of the CPT manual provides codes for use when a service or procedure is not listed. These codes typically end with "99."
- Codes for an "unlisted procedure" are found in the guidelines at the beginning of each section.
- When an unlisted procedure code is used, a special report must accompany the claim form and include:
  - Description of the service
  - The extent of the service
  - The reason it was performed
  - Equipment used
  - Amount of time and effort required

A service should not be coded as "unlisted" unless no CPT code can be found after a thorough search is done using different possibilities.

## V. Location of Service

Different procedure codes may apply to services performed in the physician's office, hospital inpatient, hospital emergency room, nursing facility, extended care facility, or the patient's home.

Always make sure to use the correct code for the place of service (POS) or location of service.

## VI. Category II Codes

- Category II codes are used to submit performance measurement activities.
- Their use facilitates data collection about quality of care.
- The use of these codes is optional.
- The codes include four digits plus a letter.

## VII. Category III Codes

- Category III codes are temporary codes used for tracking purposes.
- If a Category III code is available, it must be reported instead of an unlisted code.
- Category III codes are used to identify emerging technology, services, and procedures.
- Category III are differentiated from the Category I CPT codes by the use of an alpha-numeric character.
- New codes are added to this section semiannually via the AMA's CPT Internet site and are published annually in the CPT manual.

chapter 3

# Review Questions

## Coding and the CPT Manual

### *True/False*

***Indicate whether the sentence or statement is true or false.***

T F 1. Stand-alone codes have the full description.

T F 2. The goal of the coder is to find the code with the highest degree of accuracy to best describe the procedure performed.

T F 3. A circle or bullet indicates a new CPT code.

### *Multiple Choice*

***Identify the letter of the choice that best completes the statement or answers the question.***

4. The CPT coding system is used to report:
    a. Inpatient hospital encounters and procedures.
    b. Office and outpatient services and procedures.
    c. Both a and b.
    d. Only b.

5. CPT is divided into sections, subsections, subcategories, and individual codes. The number of and order of the sections in CPT is:
    a. Six: Medicine, Surgery, E/M, Special E/M, Pathology, Laboratory
    b. Three: Medicine, Surgery, E/M
    c. Six: E/M, Medicine, Pathology, Laboratory, Anesthesia, Surgery
    d. Six: E/M, Anesthesia, Surgery, Radiology, Pathology and Laboratory, Medicine

6. The validation for a procedure or service is provided by the ICD-9-CM (diagnosis code). However, the specific necessity for a procedure or service (in relation to the diagnosis) is provided by:
    a. Linking or matching the CPT code to its ICD-9-CM counterpart
    b. Sending the copy of the operative, procedure, or progress note with the CMS-1500 to the insurer
    c. Sequencing the CPT codes in a logical, chronological order
    d. Using specific ICD-9-CM codes for the patient's condition

7. A complete overview of all CPT modifiers is found in the CPT:
    a. Appendix B
    b. Index
    c. Appendix A
    d. Introduction

8. A black triangle to the left of a CPT code indicates that:
    a. The code has been deleted and should not be used.
    b. This is a new code never before found in CPT.
    c. This code has been revised from previous CPT publications.
    d. This code has special rules that apply to its use.

### *Completion*

***Complete each sentence or statement.***

9. CPT is revised annually and becomes effective ____________________.

10. Category III codes are considered ____________________codes.

chapter 4

# Coding Evaluation and Management Services

Evaluation and Management Services (E/M) is the coding series used to describe the services rendered by a provider that are exclusive of procedures, tests, and studies. Examples of E/M codes are office visits, inpatient consultations, and nursing facility services. There are several guidelines for determining the appropriate E/M code. Medicare allows the use of either the 1995 Documentation Guidelines or the 1997 Documentation Guidelines. Other insurance carriers may allow the use of E/M coding conventions in the CPT manual.

*NOTE: For visits and procedures performed on the same day, only bill the visit if the service provided includes a significant history, exam, and/or medical decision making. If the decision to perform the procedure was made as a result of the visit, bill both. If the visit is unrelated to the procedure, bill both. Always use a 25 modifier on the E/M service when billing both.*

## I. Overview of the Process

### A. Get the Big Picture

- Who: new or established
- Where: place of service
- What: work done
- Why: presenting problem

### B. Identify the Category and Subcategory of Service

- New patient
- Established patient
- Consultation
- Inpatient

### C. Evaluate the Components for Determining Levels of E/M Services

- History
- Examination
- Medical decision making
- Nature of presenting problem
- Time involved
- Counseling
- Coordination of care

### D. Identify the Level of Service

- Determine extent of the history obtained.
- Determine the extent of the examination performed.
- Determine the complexity of the medical decision making.

### E. Select the E/M Service

## II. General Rules of E/M Coding

### A. Office/Outpatient Visits (99201—99215)

- Not used for patient in observation area.
- Cannot be billed on the same day as a hospital or nursing facility admission.
- New patient (99201–99205)
  - Used for patients who have not received face-to-face professional services from the same physician within the last 3 years.
  - In a group practice, a patient is considered "new" to a physician if the patient has not been seen by another physician of the group who is in the same specialty in the last 3 years.
- Established patient (99211–99215)
  - Used for patients who have been seen by the physician or a member of the group within the last 3 years.
  - When patient's insurance changes, do not bill new patient code.
  - Only one E/M service per day per physician is allowed.

### B. Hospital Observation Services (99217—99220)

- Does not have to be in an "observation area."
- Key factor is how the hospital designates the patient.
- Doctor's charges should match hospital's designation.
- Encounters by physician other than admitting physician should be coded using office or outpatient consultation codes (99214–99245).
- Only one code can be billed per day.

- Do not use on the day patient is admitted to inpatient status.
- All services performed on the same date at other sites but related to the "observation" are included in code.
- Use 99217—observation care discharge day—if patient is discharged any day subsequent to the initial date of observation.
- Observation status is limited to 48 hours.

## C. Hospital Inpatient Services (99221—99233)

- Initial inpatient service
    - For use by admitting physician. Other physicians use consultation or subsequent care code.
    - If the patient is admitted after being seen in the ER, observation, or office, two services cannot be billed.
    - If physician has done a comprehensive work-up several days prior to admission and has charged comprehensive—the lowest level of admission should be reported.
    - Can be billed one time per admit by admitting physician.
- Subsequent hospital care (99231–99233)
    - Daily hospital visits, including:
        - Reviewing the medical record
        - Reviewing results of diagnostic studies
        - Reviewing change in patient status

  *NOTE: Most third-party payers will expect each of several physicians to be managing different medical problems.*

## D. Observation Services, Including Admission and Discharge on the Same Day (99234—99236)

- If the patient is admitted as an inpatient after observation, on the same day, bill only the hospital admission.
- If the patient receives other services and then is admitted to observation status, bill only observation care.

## E. Hospital Discharge Service (99238—99239)

- Final day of multiple-day hospital stay.
- 99238—30 minutes or less.
- 99239—more than 30 minutes.
- Includes:
    - Discussion of the hospital stay.
    - Instruction for continuing care.
    - Preparation of discharge records.
    - Total duration of time spent for final hospital discharge.
- Not to be used for a patient admitted and discharged the same day.

  *NOTE: You can bill for both discharge from hospital and nursing home admission on the same day (includes "swing beds—medical").*

## F. Office and Other Outpatient Consultations (99241–99245)

- Used for new or established patients.
- There must be documentation of a request for an evaluation and opinion by another physician.
- Used for consultations in office, clinic, and emergency room.
- There are no follow-up office consultations. Use established patient office visit codes (99211–99215).
- If the attending physician requests additional advice/opinion regarding the same or a new problem and the request is documented in the patient's medical record, an office consultation may be used again (send documentation with claim).

  *NOTE: Patient cannot request a consultation; it must be requested by another physician.*

## G. Inpatient Consultations (99251–99263)

- New or established patient.
- Used for services to patients in hospital or skilled nursing facility.
- Only one per admission, per specialty.

  *NOTE: The Follow-up Inpatient Consultation and Confirmatory Consultation codes were deleted as of 2006. In 2007, the consultation code series 99251–99255 was revised to remove the word "initial" from the CPT descriptor.*

## H. Emergency Department Services (99281–99288)

- Used by all physicians for services performed in the ER other than consultations.
- Used for both new and established patients. There is no distinction between the two.
- Emergency department is defined as an organized hospital-based facility for the provision of unscheduled episodic services to patients who present for immediate medical evaluation and must be available 24 hours a day.
- If critical care is required upon presentation to the ER, only critical care codes can be submitted. ER codes will not be paid for the same day.
- Not to be used for patients in observation area of hospital.

## I. Telephone/Online Evaluations (99441–99444)

Starting in 2008, several new codes have been added to CPT for telephone and on-line evaluations (non–face-to-face physician telephone services). CPT codes 99371–99373 have been deleted. See the Medicine section of the CPT for new non–face-to-face nonphysician services (codes 98966–98968).

**99441** A telephone evaluation and management services provided by a physician to an established patient, parent, or guardian not originating from a related E/M service provided within the previous 7 days nor leading to an E/M service or procedure with the next 24 hours or soonest available appointment; 5–10 minutes of discussion.

**99442** Physician telephone evaluation for 11–20 minutes of medical discussion.

**99443** Physician telephone evaluation for 21–30 minutes of medical discussion

CMS has assigned a status indicator of "N" for noncovered to these codes. This means that Medicare will not provide payment if these codes are reported. CMS has listed relative value units

(RVUs) for these codes in the 2008 Medicare physician fee schedule. The RVUs could potentially be used by private payers in valuing and reimbursing for telephone services.

**99444** Online E/M service to a patient using the Internet or similar electronic communications network. This code can only be reported with an established patient and the patient must be the one to initiate inquiry. Reportable services involve the physician's personal timely response to the patient's inquiry and must involve permanent storage (electronic or hard copy) of the encounter. The code is also assigned an "N" for noncovered status.

### J. Medical Conference Codes (99366—99368)

In 2008, several new medical team conference codes were added to CPT. CPT codes 99361–99362 have been deleted.

**99366** Medical team conference with an interdisciplinary team of health care professionals, face-to-face with the patient and/or family for 30 minutes or more.

**99367** Medical team conference where the patient or family is not present and there is participation by a physician.

**99368** Medical team conference with participation by a qualified nonphysician health care professional.

## III. Medical Clearance for Surgery

- If the physician performs his or her own history and physical (H&P), it is included in the payment for the procedure.
- Surgeon asks another physician:
  - In office—office consult
  - In hospital—inpatient consult
- Primary care physician can bill a consult if it meets criteria of consultation.
- Cannot bill consult if he or she will be responsible for care of any condition(s) during hospitalization.
- Can bill consult for medical clearance if a condition arises subsequent to admission that requires primary care physician to step in and manage.

## IV. Consultation Coding Tips

Detailed information on the CMS consultation policy may be found in the Medicare Claims Processing Manual Chapter 12—Physicians/Non-physician Practitioners 30.6.10—Consultation Services (Codes 99241–99255).

- A consultation is a service provided by a physician at the request of another physician or other appropriate source for the further evaluation and management of a patient.
- If a consulting physician initiates a diagnostic or therapeutic service at the request of the attending physician, the service still qualifies as a consultation.
- Once the consulting physician assumes responsibility for the patient's continuing care, any subsequent service rendered by that physician is not a consultation.

- Once the consulting physician takes over the care, the patient has been referred to the consulting physician and now becomes his or her patient for the total treatment of the problem.
- "Referral" means transfer of care. "Consultation" means services provided to render an opinion.
- Concurrent care is care of a patient by two or more physicians (usually of different specialties) who are acting in conjunction with each other. The consulting physician has not taken over complete care of the patient but assumes care regarding that portion for which he or she is qualified by specialty.
- If the patient is referred for treatment or for a diagnostic procedure, the service is a visit (new, established, or subsequent hospital) not a consultation.
- The current policy on consultations and treatment on the same day is that the physician can initiate treatment and still bill that visit as a consultation. A transfer of care does not occur until the referring physician "transfers responsibility for the patient's complete care." Previously, the policy stated "partial or complete care." Program transmittal 1644 reversed Medicare Carriers Manual 15506.
- The three major requirements of a consultation as included in the Medicare Carriers Manual, Section B3, 15506 are:
  - A consultation is distinguished from a visit because it is provided by a physician whose opinion or advice regarding evaluation and/or management of a specific problem is requested by another physician or appropriate source (unless it is a patient-generated confirmatory consultation).
  - A request for a consultation from an appropriate source and the need for consultation must be documented in the patient's medical record and included in the requesting provider's documentation.
  - After the consultation is provided, the consultant prepares a written report, which is separate from the medical record documentation, of his or her findings that is provided to the requesting physician.

## V. Preventive Medicine

Preventive medicine (PM) describes services rendered to a patient in the absence of complaints. Examples include:

- Routine physical exam or check-up
- Visit preceding a screening colonoscopy

These are used only if the patient has no symptoms or abnormal findings. If at the time of the PM visit the doctor does counseling and/or risk-reduction intervention, use codes 99401–99429 in addition to the PM codes.

# Summary E/M Worksheet

**Location of Service:**

| | | |
|---|---|---|
| ______ Office/outpatient | ______ Office/consult | ______ ER |
| ______ Init/hosp | ______ Sub hospital | ______ Discharge |
| ______ Init NH | ______ Sub NH | |

**Patient Status:**

______ New patient ______ Established patient

**Requesting Physician:**

______ Yes ______ No

**History:**

| | |
|---|---|
| ______ Problem focused | Chief complaint, brief history of problem |
| ______ Expanded problem focused | + Problem pertinent to system review |
| ______ Detailed | CC, extended history, extended ROS, pertinent PMH/FH/SH |
| ______ Comprehensive | CC, extended history, complete ROS, complete PMH/FH/SH |

**Exam:**

| | |
|---|---|
| ______ Problem focused | Affected body area or organ system |
| ______ Expanded problem focused | + Other related systems |
| ______ Detailed | Extended exam of affected/extended body area/organ system |
| ______ Comprehensive | Complete single-system specialty exam or multi-system exam |

**Medical Decision Making:**

| **Elements** | **A** | **B** | **C** | **D** |
|---|---|---|---|---|
| Number diagnosis and management options | Minimal | Limited | Multiple | Extensive |
| Amount/complexity of data reviewed | Minimal | Limited | Moderate | Extensive |
| Risk complications morbidity/mortality | Minimal | Low | Moderate | High |

| | |
|---|---|
| Straightforward | ⅔ column A elements met |
| Low complexity | ⅔ column B elements met |
| Moderate complexity | ⅔ column C elements met |
| High complexity | ⅔ column D elements met |

Time must be documented only if greater than 50% of face-to-face time with patient is in counseling/coordination of care. Utilization of time as a determinant of level of service is an unusual situation for new patients or consults because the documentation of history, physical examination, and decision making should reflect the level of visit billed. However, on follow-up visits, time would probably be billed for counseling and coordination of care. The Documentation Guidelines for Evaluation and Management Services do not provide an index of time equating to a specific level of service.

chapter 4

# Review Questions

## Coding Evaluation and Management (E/M) Services

*Indicate whether the sentence or statement is true or false.*

T F 1. The E/M level of service reflects the amount of work involved in providing health care to patients.

T F 2. Observation services are furnished in a hospital inpatient setting to determine whether the patient needs further treatment.

T F 3. A second opinion requested by a patient, not at the request of another physician, is considered a consultation.

T F 4. Key components of an E/M code are history, examination, and medical decision making.

T F 5. The terms *consultation* and *referral* are generally synonymous.

*Identify the letter of the choice that best completes the statement or answers the question.*

6. Where is the E/M section located in the CPT text?
   a. It is the first CPT section found after the introduction.
   b. CPT is organized numerically; therefore, it is the last section of CPT.
   c. It has its own subsection in the Medicine section.
   d. It is the section following Anesthesia.

7. For an established patient with a history level of expanded problem focused, the examination is expanded problem focused and the medical decision making is of low complexity. What is the correct code?
   a. 99211
   b. 99213
   c. 99212
   d. 99214

*Complete each sentence or statement.*

8. For a new patient 99203, the history level is ____________________, the examination is ____________________, and the medical decision making is of ____________________ complexity.

9. __________________ means transfer of care. __________________means care provided to render an opinion.

10. Three things must happen for a visit to be a consultation. They are __________________, __________________, and __________________.

chapter 5

# Coding Anesthesia Services

## I. General Concepts

Anesthesia must be administered by, or under the supervision of, a physician.
Anesthesia services may involve:

- General
- Regional
- Supplementation of local anesthesia

The service includes:

- Preoperative visits
- Postoperative visits
- Anesthesia care during procedure
- Administration of fluids and/or blood, incident to the anesthesia or surgery
- Monitoring procedures

Unusual forms of monitoring not bundled into the anesthesia codes are:

- Intra-arterial
- Central venous
- Swan-Ganz

The most common source of anesthesia nomenclature used to report anesthesia is CPT and the Relative Value Guide (RVG) published by the American Society of Anesthesiologists (ASA).

Anesthesia reimbursement is calculated by adding time units to base units and multiplying by a conversion factor. The conversion factor varies by region.

A "unit" of time is usually 10 or 15 minutes.

Depending on the requirements of the specific insurance company, an anesthesia crosswalk may be necessary.

The CPT codes are 00100–01999. The 5-digit codes, plus modifier codes, are used to report services involving the administration of anesthesia. Anesthesia codes are grouped anatomically by area.

The RVG provides the same list but also includes the base units associated with each procedure.

Many providers use the CPT surgical code to report anesthesia. Unless specifically required by the payer, it is recommended to use the more specific CPT anesthesia codes.

Several surgical CPT codes cross over to a single anesthesia code.

When anesthesia services are provided for procedures that normally do not require anesthesia, there must be documentation indicating the condition(s) or reason(s) for the anesthesia services (e.g., confusion, unstable condition). The reason does not have to be submitted with the claim but MUST be kept in the record and available on request.

Only one anesthesia code is listed per operative session for anesthesia reimbursement.

In the event that more than one procedure is performed, choose the anesthesia/surgical code associated with the highest base limit.

Other services can be reported on the same date of service, such as qualifying circumstances and central venous or arterial access.

## II. Anesthesia Modifiers and Qualifying Circumstances

Two of the most common modifiers are physical status (PS; P1–P6) and qualifying circumstances (99100–99140).

The qualifying circumstances are not technical modifiers but an adjunct means of identifying services.

Modifiers may be added to the primary code to identify services rendered beyond the primary code description. Medicare and Medicaid require modifiers for unusual anesthesia services.

PS modifiers have common descriptions. Some PS modifiers and the qualifying circumstances add base units to the calculation for anesthesia reimbursement.

The following are the PS modifiers that can be used to identify the patient requiring anesthesia:

**P1** A normal, healthy patient.

**P2** A patient with mild systemic disease.

**P3** A patient with severe systemic disease.

**P4** A patient with severe systemic disease that is a constant threat to life.

**P5** A moribund patient who is not expected to survive without the operation.

**P6** A declared brain-dead patient whose organs are removed for donor purposes.

Qualifying circumstances also have common descriptions throughout the reimbursement industry. Such services are considered "add-on" services, and therefore a 51 modifier is not required.

**99100** Anesthesia for a patient of extreme age, under 1 year or over 70 years.

**99116** Anesthesia complicated by utilization of total body hypothermia.

**99135** Anesthesia complicated by utilization of controlled hypotension.

**99140** Anesthesia complicated by emergency conditions (specify).

*NOTE: An emergency is defined as a situation that exists that would lead to significant increase in the threat to life or body part if there were a delay in treatment.*

# III. Unbundling and Specialized Anesthesia Services

Unbundling or fragmented billing of anesthesia services is defined as billing for procedures that are already included in the definition of the basic value (global package).

Included in the basic value are:

- Usual preoperative and postoperative visits
- Initial set-up of ventilation assistance and management service (on the same day of service)
- Initiation of pain management therapy, contingent on mode (same-day surgery)
- Anesthesiologist's history of the patient
- Administration of fluids
- Routine venipuncture
- Intravenous (IV) infusion therapy
- Administration of most IV medications and drugs
- Blood/platelet administration
- Anesthesia care during the procedure
- Routine intubation
- Placement of nasogastric (N/G) tube

# IV. Usual Monitoring Services

- Vital signs (blood pressure [BP])
- Temperature
- Oximetry (pulse oximetry)
- Capnography ($CO_2$ monitoring)
- Mass spectrometry (measurement of wave length of light)
- Electrocardiography (EKG/ECG)
- Electroencephalogram (EEG)
- Somatosensory testing

# V. Specialized Services

Specialized services must be reasonable and necessary and not included in the global surgery fee.

In general, most payers allow additional benefits for Swan-Ganz catheters, arterial lines, and central venous pressure lines placed by the attending anesthesiologist at the time of basic anesthesia service.

# VI. Requirements

- The service must be requested by the attending physician and be made known to the patient.
- The service must include:
  - Performance of a preanesthetic examination and evaluation
  - Prescription of the anesthesia care required

  - Personal participation in, or medical direction of, the entire plan of care
  - Continuous physical presence of the anesthesiologist or, in the case of medical direction (Medicare only), of the resident or nurse anesthetist being medically directed
  - Proximate presence or (in the case of medical direction) availability of the anesthesiologist for diagnosis or treatment of emergencies
- All institutional regulations pertaining to anesthesia services must be observed, and all the usual services performed by the anesthesiologist must be furnished, including, but not limited to, the following:
  - Usual noninvasive cardiocirculatory and respiratory monitoring
  - Oxygen administration, when indicated
  - Intravenous administration of sedatives, tranquilizers, antiemetics, narcotics, other analgesics, beta-blockers, vasopressors, bronchodilators, antihypertensives, or other pharmacologic therapy as may be required in the judgment of the anesthesiologist

## VII. Anesthesia Time

The time when anesthesia services begin and end must be calculated uniformly. Anesthesia time starts when the anesthesiologist begins to prepare the patient for the procedure.

Anesthesia time stops when the anesthesiologist's care of the patient is over and the patient care is turned over to postanesthesia care unit (PACU) staff and the anesthesiologist's constant attendance is no longer required.

Time spent performing procedures such as arterial line insertion or Swan-Ganz catheterization is not calculated; the rationale is that those services will be billed in addition to the anesthesia service.

## VIII. Moderate Sedation Codes (99143—99150)

The previous conscious sedation codes 99141 and 99142 were deleted from CPT in 2006.

Moderate (conscious) sedation is defined as a drug-induced depression of consciousness during which patients respond purposefully to verbal commands, either alone or accompanied by light tactile stimulation. No interventions are required to maintain a patent airway, and spontaneous ventilation is adequate. Cardiovascular function is usually maintained.

Moderate sedation does not include minimal sedation (anxiolysis), deep sedation, or monitored anesthesia care (00100–01999). When providing moderate sedation, the following services are included and are not reported separately:

- Assessment of the patient
- Establishment of IV access and fluids to maintain patency
- Administration of agents
- Maintenance of sedation
- Monitoring of oxygen saturation, heart rate, and blood pressure
- Recovery

Intraservice time starts with the administration of the sedation agent(s), requires continuous face-to-face attendance, and ends at the conclusion of personal contact by the physician providing the sedation.

*NOTE: Moderate sedation is inherent to any endoscopic service that is listed in Appendix G of CPT with a "bull's-eye," which indicates that sedation is bundled into the value for the procedure and is not reported separately.*

**99143** Moderate sedation services (other than those services described by codes 00100–01999) provided by the same physician performing the diagnostic or therapeutic service that the sedation supports, requiring the presence of an independent trained observer to assist in the monitoring of the patient's level of consciousness and physiological status; under 5 years of age, first 30 minutes intraservice time.

**99144** Moderate sedation services (other than those services described by codes 00100–01999) provided by the same physician performing the diagnostic or therapeutic service that the sedation supports, requiring the presence of an independent trained observer to assist in the monitoring of the patient's level of consciousness and physiological status; age 5 years or older, first 30 minutes intraservice time.

**99145** Moderate sedation services (other than those services described by codes 00100–01999) provided by the same physician performing the diagnostic or therapeutic service that the sedation supports, requiring the presence of an independent trained observer to assist in the monitoring of the patient's level of consciousness and physiological status; each additional 15 minutes intraservice time (list separately in addition to code for primary service).

**99148** Moderate sedation services (other than those services described by codes 00100–01999) provided by a physician other than the health care professional performing the diagnostic or therapeutic service that the sedation supports; under 5 years of age, first 30 minutes intraservice time.

**99149** Moderate sedation services (other than those services described by codes 00100–01999) provided by a physician other than the health care professional performing the diagnostic or therapeutic service that the sedation supports; age 5 years or older, first 30 minutes intraservice time.

**99150** Moderate sedation services (other than those services described by codes 00100–01999) provided by a physician other than the health care professional performing the diagnostic or therapeutic service that the sedation supports; each additional 15 minutes intraservice time (list separately in addition to code for primary service).

chapter 5

# Review Questions

## Coding Anesthesia Services

***Indicate whether the sentence or statement is true or false.***

T F 1. An anesthesia "unit" of time is usually 10–15 minutes.

T F 2. Anesthesia codes are grouped anatomically by area.

T F 3. Anesthesia qualifying circumstances are technical modifiers.

***Complete each sentence or statement.***

4. Anesthesia services are broken into (but not limited to) 3 categories: ____________________, ____________________, and ____________________.

5. Two of the most common anesthesia modifiers are ____________________ and ____________________.

chapter 6

# Coding Surgical Procedures

## I. General Guidelines

The surgery section of CPT includes two types of procedures: major (global) and diagnostic and other minor procedures.

To select the CPT surgical code that accurately reflects the service performed:

- Read the surgical code description carefully.
- Remember that modifiers may have a significant impact on reimbursement.
  *NOTE: Just because there is a CPT code describing a procedure does not mean that payers will reimburse for that service.*

## II. Surgical Package (Global Surgery)

The surgical package includes the normal, uncomplicated performance of specific surgical services, with the assumption that "on average all surgical procedures of a given type are similar with respect to skill-level, duration, and length of normal follow-up care."

- Services bundled into the global surgical package apply only to services provided by the surgeon and assistant surgeon.
- Preoperative services:
  - Include all preoperative visits in or out of the hospital the day of or the day before surgery.
  - Lab work/X-rays can be billed separately if performed in the office prior to surgery.
  - Include the admission H&P.
  - The initial patient visit/consult during which the need for surgery is determined can be billed separately with a 57 modifier.
- The global surgery package includes intraoperative services that are a usual and necessary part of surgery.

- Postoperative services are all services performed by the surgeon for 10 or 90 days post-op, whichever applies, and are included in the global package, unless:
  - The problem is unrelated to the diagnosis for which surgery was performed.
  - Involves a different diagnosis than that for original service.
  - Involves an added treatment other than normal recovery from surgery. (Immunosuppressive therapy following transplants is not included and is paid separately.)
  - Additional payment is made for reoperation in the OR dealing with complications of the original surgery.
  - For reoperation where no CPT code exists for the procedure, payment may not exceed 50% of the value of intraoperative services originally performed.

  *NOTE: No service performed by the surgeon within the 10 or 90 days post-op period will be paid without a modifier.*
- Medicare does not pay for services related to complications of surgery unless the complication requires a return trip to the OR.

# III. Unbundling/Fragmenting

- Unbundling:
  - The global surgery package includes preoperative, intraoperative, and postoperative services. The physician is not allowed to bill separately for the various parts of the global package.
  - For Medicare, the global fee for office surgery also includes all supplies, which may not be billed separately.
- Fragmenting: All surgical procedures are made up of various steps:
  - Operative approach (incision, scope)
  - Each segment of the surgery itself
  - Closure of the operative wound

  *NOTE: Each step cannot be coded and billed separately.*
- Notation "(Separate procedure)" at the end of the code description is your warning that this code is a part of, or one step, in a larger procedure and cannot be used unless that procedure was the only one performed at that time.
- In the case where the surgeon does not know what is wrong with the patient and has to explore first, once inside and the problem is discovered and repaired, the exploration is not charged separately. The CPT code represents the final procedure performed.
- The following procedures can only be coded if they are all that is done at the operative session. If they lead to further surgery, they become part of that surgery and are not coded separately:
  - Endoscopy
  - Arthroscopy
  - Craniotomy
  - Cystourethroscopy
  - Colposcopy
  - Laryngoscopy

- If several procedures are performed using an endoscopic approach, each code contains reimbursement of the scope; therefore, reimbursement will be reduced by the amount of the basic scope procedure for all but the most expensive procedure.
- Add-on codes: Some of the listed procedures are commonly carried out or performed in addition to the primary procedure. All add-on codes are exempt from the multiple procedure rules in CPT. Add-on codes do not require the use of the 51 modifier.

# IV. Diagnostic Services

- Most diagnostic services do not have a global package.
- Diagnostic services may be performed in addition to consultative services.
- Diagnostic services are performed to determine or establish a patient's diagnosis.
- They include performance of the procedure and recovery of the patient after the procedure.
- Additional care of the underlying disease or injury may be coded separately.

# V. Endoscopic Procedures

- Endoscopic procedures are performed through an existing orifice. The procedure is considered diagnostic when the scope is placed into a body cavity to visualize an abnormality or to determine the extent of a disease.
- When the endoscope is placed for visualization and a therapeutic procedure is performed, the procedure is no longer considered diagnostic.
- Guidelines for billing endoscopic procedures:
  - A diagnostic endoscopy is billed only when performed alone.
  - The diagnostic endoscopic procedure is incidental to the therapeutic endoscopic procedure.
  - A diagnostic endoscopy can be billed when it leads to incisional therapeutic services.
  - When an endoscopic procedure, other than a diagnostic or screening colonoscopy, with full preparation has been aborted or is incomplete, use modifier 52 (reduced service) to identify this service.
  - For a diagnostic or screening colonoscopy that is aborted, use modifier 53.
- Endoscopic procedures are classified as zero day global fees.

# VI. Materials Supplied by the Physician

- Can bill for supplies and services over and above those usually included with the office visit or service rendered (99070).
- Do not bill supplies that are customarily included in surgical packages (gauze, sponges, applicators).
- Attach a statement to the claim form for extraordinary expensive supplies (stents, etc).

## VII. Biopsy Services

- Use biopsy codes to report the removal of a small amount of tissue to determine the extent of a disease, or to confirm a diagnosis.
- Biopsy codes are appropriate for needle aspiration for biopsy, incisional biopsy, and partial excision, as well as for scraping, curetting, and a skin punch.
- Biopsy codes are arranged in the surgery section of the CPT by anatomical location of the lesion or cyst.
- Use integumentary codes when the biopsy is of skin and subcutaneous tissue only.
- You cannot code for a biopsy and an excision of the same lesion.

## VIII. Laser Surgery

- When the use of a laser significantly alters the procedure performed, use a code that specifically identifies laser in the description.
- Generally, laser use is considered a technical function that does not significantly change the desired outcome of a primary procedure.
- "Destruction by any method" implies that the result is what the code is intending to describe, not the method of performance of the procedure.

chapter 6

# Review Questions

## Coding Surgical Procedures

***Indicate whether the sentence or statement is true or false.***

T F 1. Preoperative clearance indicates that a surgeon has requested the examination of a patient to determine whether the patient is a good surgical candidate.

T F 2. Physician standby services involve a physician spending a prolonged period of time, with patient contact, waiting for an event to occur that requires the physician's service.

T F 3. Two types of procedures in the surgery section of the CPT are: global and diagnostic.

T F 4. In surgery, all add-on codes are not exempt from the multiple procedure rule.

***Identify the letter of the choice that best completes the statement or answers the question.***

5. When the phrase "separate procedure" follows a code, that instruction applies to:
    a. That specific code only.
    b. All indented codes below.
    c. Codes with a semicolon that may follow.
    d. None of the above.

6. In a global surgery package, which of the following is not included?
    a. Initial consultation
    b. Admission H&P
    c. All services 90 days post-operative
    d. Anesthesia services performed by surgeon

***Complete each sentence or statement.***

7. When coding an excision of a lesion, the coder must know the site, ________________________ of the lesion, ________________________ of lesions, ________________________ status, and the method used for removal.

8. Surgical endoscopy always includes ________________________ endoscopy.

chapter 7

# Coding Radiology, Pathology, and Laboratory Services

## I. Radiology General Guidelines

- The code selection is determined by the number of views or studies from different angles, as well as the part of the body being x-rayed.
- Radiological tests can be broken into components or billed together as follows:
  - Technical component (TC): facility portion. Includes the use of the equipment, supplies, and employment of the technicians.
  - Professional component (PC): reading. Interpretation and report by the physician (26).
  - Global (includes both the professional and technical components).

## II. Pathology and Laboratory

- Use the 26 modifier for physician component (professional).
- Use the 22 modifier for additional time and effort or extra skill, also for special reports.
- Use the 32 modifier for mandated service, i.e., when provided service is required by payer.
- To select the appropriate code, identify the following:
  - Test performed
  - Anatomical site
  - Condition
  - Abbreviation (RBC for red blood cell)
  - Procedure or methodology
  - Procedural test group (chemistry tests, e.g., CBC, lipid panel)

## III. Therapeutic Drug Assays

- Do not confuse with qualitative "drug testing."
- Use the following guidelines:
  - Determine the purpose of an assay—qualitative or quantitative?
  - If qualitative, it simply identifies the presence or absence of a substance; use 80100–80103.

- If the assay is quantitative, look in the Chemistry section (tells how much substance is in the body for therapeutic levels).
- If no code is found in the Chemistry section, look for the code in the Therapeutic Drug Assay (TDA) section of the CPT manual.
- If no specific code is found in the TDA section and the test is for identifying drug level, use 80299.

## IV. Surgical Pathology

- If several specimens are received in the same container without separate identification, bill only one surgical pathology code.
- If several specimens are received in the same container and are identified separately, bill each specimen separately.
- If several specimen bottles are received, bill per specimen using applicable codes for each, based on anatomical site.

## V. Frozen Sections

- Use 88331 for a frozen section from a single specimen. If frozen sections are performed on two separate specimens, use 88331 × 2.

  *NOTE: Always make sure the diagnosis matches the test being performed.*

chapter 7

# Review Questions

## Coding Radiology, Pathology, and Laboratory Services

***Indicate whether the sentence or statement is true or false.***

T F 1. In therapeutic drug assays, to determine the purpose of an assay, you need to know if it is qualitative or quantitative.

***Complete each sentence or statement.***

2. The technical component of an examination covers the use of the ______________________, supplies, and employment of the ______________________________.

3. The number of ________________________ or studies from different angles determines the code selection in many radiological procedures.

4. The _____________ modifier is used in radiology, pathology, and laboratory services to indicate the professional component.

chapter 8

# Coding from the Medicine Section of CPT

## I. General Concepts

The Medicine section of the CPT manual contains procedures for the following:

- Evaluation
- Treatment
- Diagnosis

When E/M services are performed and indicate the necessity for other diagnostic procedures, it is appropriate to code both.

The Medicine section can be used in conjunction with all other sections of CPT. It includes codes for the following:

- Immunizations
- Injections
- Therapeutic or diagnostic infusion
- Psychiatric services
- Dialysis
- Gastroenterology
- Ophthalmology
- Otorhinolaryngology (ENT)
- Cardiac services and studies
- Pulmonary
- Allergy
- Neurology
- Chemotherapy
- Dermatology
- Restorative medicine
- Other special services

## II. Immunizations

- Immune globulin administration is often used to provide passive immunity to individuals exposed to a disease where no active immunity has been established or administered.

**90471** Single doses of a vaccine or toxoid and/or administration of one combination dose of a vaccine or toxoid.

**90472** Administration of multiple, single or combination vaccines and/or toxoids.

- Both administration codes encompass a variety of routes of administration:
  - Intranasal
  - Oral
  - Percutaneous
  - Intradermal
  - Intramuscular
  - Jet injection
- Both codes may be billed with an E/M service.
- The E/M service must be a separately documented service.

## III. Therapeutic, Prophylactic, and Diagnostic Injections and Infusions (90765—90799)

A therapeutic, prophylactic, or diagnostic IV infusion or injection is for the administration of substances and drugs. The fluid used to administer the drug in incidental hydration is not separately reportable.

These services typically require direct physician supervision for patient assessment, provision of consent, safety oversight, and intraservice supervision of staff. Typically, such infusions require:

- Special consideration to prepare, dose, or dispose of
- Training, practice, and competency for staff who administer the infusions
- Periodic patient assessment with vital sign monitoring during the infusion

An intravenous or intra-arterial push is an injection in which the health care professional who administers the drug is continuously present to administer the injection and observe the patient, or an infusion of 15 minutes or less.

- Use when materials other than vaccines or toxins are injected.
- Not for allergy immunotherapy or chemotherapy.
- Method of delivery is pertinent.

**90765** Intravenous infusion; initial, up to one (1) hour.

**90766** Intravenous infusion; each additional hour, up to eight (8) hours; list separately in addition to code for primary procedure.

**90767** Additional sequential infusion, up to one (1) hour; list separately in addition to code for primary procedure.

**90768** Concurrent infusion; list separately in addition to code for primary procedure.

**90769** Subcutaneous infusion for therapy or prophylaxis (specify substance or drug); initial, up to one (1) hour, including pump set-up and establishment of subcutaneous infusion site(s).

**90770** Subcutaneous infusion for therapy or prophylaxis (specify substance or drug), each additional hour; list separately in addition to code for primary procedure.

**90771** Subcutaneous infusion for therapy or prophylaxis (specify substance or drug), additional pump set-up with establishment of new subcutaneous infusion site(s); list separately in addition to code for primary procedure.

**90772** Subcutaneous (Sub-Q) or intramuscular (IM) injection.

**90773** Intra-arterial injection.

**90774** Intravenous (IV) push, single or initial substance/drug.

**90775** Each additional sequential intravenous push of a new substance/drug; list separately in addition to code for primary procedure.

**90779** Unlisted therapeutic, prophylactic, or diagnostic intravenous or intra-arterial injection or infusion or all other types of therapeutic or diagnostic injections not listed.

## IV. Hydration

The physician work related to hydration, injection, and infusion services predominantly involves affirmation of the treatment plan and direct supervision of staff. If a significantly separately identifiable E/M service is performed, the appropriate E/M service code should be reported using modifier 25 in addition to coding for the service.

Hydration services describe a prepackaged fluid and electrolytes but are not used to report infusion of drugs or other substances. Hydration IV infusions typically require direct physician supervision for purposes of consent, safety oversight, or intraservice supervision of staff. Typically, such infusions require little special handling to prepare or dispose of, and staff who administer these do not typically require advanced practice training. After initial set-up, infusion typically entails little patient risk and thus little monitoring.

**90760** Intravenous infusion, hydration, initial, up to one (1) hour.

**90761** Intravenous infusion, hydration, each additional hour, up to eight (8) hours; list separately in addition to code for the primary procedure.

## V. Gastroenterology

- Includes both therapeutic and diagnostic procedures.
- Endoscopic procedures are located in the Surgical section of CPT.
- Duodenal intubation and aspiration services are listed in the Laboratory section.

**89100** Duodenal intubation and aspiration, single specimen.

**89105** Duodenal intubation and aspiration with collection of multiple fractional specimens with pancreatic or gallbladder stimulation.

- Gastric intubation and aspiration services are listed in the Laboratory section.

**89130** Gastric intubation and aspiration, each specimen.

**89132** Gastric intubation and aspiration, after stimulation.

**89135** Gastric intubation, aspiration, and fractional collections, such as for a gastric secretory study, one (1) hour.

**89136** Gastric intubation, aspiration, and fractional collections, for two (2) hours.

**89140** Gastric intubation, aspiration, and fractional collections for two (2) hours, including gastric stimulation by substances such as histalog or pentagastrin.

**89141** Gastric intubation, aspiration, and fractional collections for three (3) hours, including gastric stimulation.

### *Occult Blood Testing*

**82270** Blood, occult, by peroxidase activity (e.g., guaiac study), qualitative; feces, consecutive collected specimens with a single determination, for colorectal neoplasm screening.

**82271** Blood, occult, by peroxidase activity, of sources other than feces.

**82272** Blood, occult, by peroxidase activity (e.g., guaiac study), qualitative; feces, 1–3 simultaneous determinations, for other than colorectal neoplasm screening.

**82274** Blood, occult, by fecal hemoglobin determination by immunoassay, qualitative, feces, 1–3 simultaneous determinations.

**G0394** Blood occult test (e.g., guaiac), feces, for single determination for colorectal neoplasm (e.g., patient was provided three cards or one triple card for consecutive collections).

## VI. Neurostimulator Codes (95980—95982)

These codes were added in 2008 to report electronic analysis and programming services provided for and specific to gastric neurostimulator pulse generator or transmitter codes. The typical patient for codes 95981 and 95982 is a follow-up patient.

**95980** Electronic analysis of implanted neurostimulator pulse generator system (e.g., rate, pulse amplitude and duration, configuration of wave form, battery status, electrode selectability, output modulation, cycling, impedance, and patient measurements) gastric neurostimulator pulse generator/transmitter; intraoperative, with programming.

**95981** Subsequent, without reprogramming.

**95982** Subsequent, with reprogramming.

## VII. Special Services and Reports

**99024** Postoperative visit during global surgical services.

## VIII. Telephone Services (98966—98968)

New in 2008, CPT has added codes for non–face-to-face nonphysician telephone services. See codes 99441–99443 used for non–face-to-face physician telephone services.

**98966** Telephone assessment and management service provided by a qualified nonphysician health care professional to an established patient for 5–10 minutes of medical discussion.

**98967** Nonphysician telephone assessment and management service for 11–20 minutes of medical discussion.

**98968** Nonphysician telephone assessment and management services for 21–30 minutes of medical discussion.

Similar to codes 99441–99443, CMS has assigned an "N" for noncovered status to these codes.

chapter 8

# Review Questions

## Coding from the Medicine Section of CPT

***Indicate whether the sentence or statement is true or false.***

T F 1. The Medicine section of CPT contains procedures for evaluation, therapeutic, and diagnostic services.

T F 2. It is not appropriate to bill an E/M service with procedures from the Medicine section.

T F 3. The Medicine section cannot be used in conjunction with all other sections of CPT manual.

T F 4. Gastroenterology codes are typically endoscopic, but in the Medicine section of CPT gastroenterology codes can be found for testing purposes.

***Identify the letter of the choice that best completes the statement or answers the question.***

5. In the Medicine section of the CPT, there are many divisions and specialty areas known as:
    a. Minisections
    b. Subsections
    c. Specialty categories
    d. Subcategories

6. Which of the following is not considered a preventive visit?
    a. Yearly OB/GYN visit
    b. Service rendered in absence of complaint
    c. Dialysis
    d. Visit to weigh a normal newborn

7. Which of the following are routes for the administration of immunizations?
    a. Intranasal
    b. Percutaneous
    c. Intramuscular
    d. All of the above

# Coding Conventions

chapter 9

# Using Modifiers Effectively

## I. General Concepts

A modifier is a 2-digit number or two letters that "modifies" or alters the CPT or HCPCS code and gives the reason payment should be adjusted from the usual payment for that procedure code.

- A short version of CPT modifiers appears on the inside cover of the CPT book, with the long version in Appendix A.
- The HCPCS modifiers are included in Appendix A of the HCPCS book.
- Eight key reasons why modifiers are utilized with CPT codes:
  - A service or procedure has both a professional and a technical component.
  - A service is performed by more than one physician and/or in more than one location.
  - A service has been increased or reduced.
  - Only part of a service was performed.
  - An adjunctive service was performed.
  - A service or procedure was provided more than once.
  - Unusual events occurred.
  - A service was provided during a global period but is not included as part of the global reimbursement.
- CPT allows two ways for modifiers to be used:
  - A 2-digit number attached to the procedure code.
  - A 5-digit modifier (09922).

  *NOTE: Most carriers prefer the 2-digit modifier.*
- Modifiers 54, 55, and 56 cover situations where the surgeon does not provide all the medical care related to the surgery. Physicians, other than the surgeon, may provide and be paid for medical care related to the surgery if the surgeon indicates his service does not include the preoperative or postoperative medical care.
- Any complications that arise during the surgical procedure/operative session are not to be separately billable according to both NCCI and Medicare guidelines. If the time to repair the complications is excessive, modifier 22 can be applied to the main procedure,

and the claim would be reviewed. If the patient is taken back to the OR to treat the complications, modifier 78 would be applied to that/those procedure(s).

- Therapeutic surgery includes all related medical care. The modifier 24 is used when there is a separate, postoperative medical service, unrelated to the surgical procedure.

  Example: A patient had surgery last week but now comes to the office for an acute flare of Crohn's disease. If the flare of the Crohn's disease is not related to the surgery, the office visit may be billed as a separate service using the modifier 24.

Modifiers increase in importance each year. Each new edition of CPT and HCPCS brings changes to the familiar ones in addition to new modifiers. Be certain to review the modifier sections when you look for changes in procedure codes.

Review Appendix A of your current CPT manual for definitions of all the modifiers. It is also important to identify when the use of a modifier has been expanded or restricted by a third party payer.

## II. Definition of Modifiers

Modifiers can be thought of as adjectives. Following are the definitions of several modifiers:

**22** Revised for 2008. Increased procedural service; service is greater than described in the CPT manual. When the work required to provide a service is substantially greater than typically required, it may be identified by adding modifier 22 to the usual procedure code. Documentation must support the substantial additional work and the reason for the additional work (i.e., increased intensity or time, technical difficulty of procedure, severity of patient's condition, physical and mental effort required). Whenever billing modifier 22, include the procedure report as well as an additional paragraph explaining the need for additional time or work with the claim.

**25** Revised for 2008. Significant, separately identifiable evaluation and management service by the same physician on the same day of the procedure or other service. It may be necessary to indicate that on the day a procedure or service identified by a CPT code was performed, the patient's condition required a significant, separately identifiable E/M service above and beyond the other service provided or beyond the usual preoperative and postoperative care associated with the procedure that was performed. A significant, separately identifiable E/M service is defined or substantiated by documentation that satisfies the relevant criteria for the respective E/M service to be reported. The E/M service may be prompted by the symptom or condition for which the procedure and/or service was provided. As such, different diagnoses are not required for reporting of the E/M services on the same date. This circumstance may be reported by adding modifier 25 to the appropriate level of E/M service.

*NOTE: This modifier is not used to report an E/M service that resulted in a decision to perform surgery; see modifier 57. It should not be used for an H&P performed prior to a scheduled procedure.*

**51** Multiple procedures. When multiple procedures, other than E/M services, are performed at the same session by the same provider, the primary procedure or service may be reported as listed. The additional procedure(s) or service(s) may be identified by appending modifier 51. The National Surgery Coverage Provision states that modifier 51 should not be reported to Medicare carriers. Check with your commercial insurance carriers as to their policy on modifier 51.

**52** Reduced services. Under certain circumstances, a service or procedure is partially reduced or eliminated at the physician's discretion. Use the 52 modifier if the procedure did not meet the complete description for that code.

**53** Discontinued procedure. Under certain circumstances, the physician may elect to terminate a surgical or diagnostic procedure. Due to extenuating circumstances or those that threaten the well-being of the patient, it may be necessary to indicate that a surgical or diagnostic procedure was started but discontinued. This code is used by Medicare contractors to identify a discontinued screening colonoscopy for colorectal cancer screening payment purposes.

*NOTE: The 53 modifier is not used to report the elective cancellation of a procedure prior to the patient's anesthesia induction and/or surgical preparation in the operative suite.*

Modifiers 54, 55, and 56 are used when you see the key word "only."

**54** When one physician performs the surgical procedure only and another provides preoperative and/or postoperative management. Surgical services may be identified by adding 54 to the usual procedure code or by use of separate 5-digit modifier 09954.

**55** When one physician performs the postoperative management and another physician has performed the surgical procedure, the postoperative component may be identified by adding the modifier 55 to the usual procedure code or by the use of separate 5-digit modifier 09955.

**56** When one physician performs the preoperative care and evaluation and another physician performs the surgical procedure, the preoperative component may be identified by adding the modifier 56 to the usual procedure code or by the use of separate 5-digit modifier 09956.

**57** Decision for surgery; made within the global surgical period. Medicare pays for an evaluation and management service on the day of or on the day before a procedure with a 90-day global surgical period if the physician uses CPT modifier 57 to indicate that the service was for the decision to perform the procedure. Medicare will pay for an evaluation and management service with the CPT provided the day of or on the day before a procedure with a 0- or 10-day global surgical period with the modifier 25.

**58** Revised for 2008. Staged and/or related procedure or service by the same physician during the postoperative period. This modifier is used to indicate that the procedure or service was planned prospectively at the time of the original procedure, or staged; was more extensive than the original procedure; or was for therapy following a diagnostic surgical procedure. Do not use this modifier to report a return trip to the OR or to report any procedures related to complications from surgery.

*NOTE: Modifier 79 should not be used to report staged procedures.*

**59** Distinct procedure or service. This important NCCI-associated modifier, which is often used incorrectly, is used when multiple procedures, normally bundled under NCCI edits, are performed on different lesions of sites, i.e., two or more procedures are performed at different anatomic sites or different patient encounters. It should only be used if no other modifier more appropriately describes the relationships of the two or more procedures codes. The 59 modifier allows for payment that would have otherwise been denied.

**62** Two surgeons. Can be used when both surgeons participate equally in the same procedure, as defined by one CPT code. Both physicians must dictate a procedure report. The Medicare reimbursement is 125% of the fee schedule amount split at 62.5% for each physician. Example: PEG placement—CPT 43246.

**63** Procedures on infants weighing less than 4 kg. The weight of the child must be identified in the operative/endoscopy report in order to use this modifier. This modifier allows for increased reimbursement by the payers.

**76** Repeat procedure by the same physician. The same physician may need to indicate that a procedure or service was repeated subsequent to the original procedure or service.

**77** Repeat procedure by another physician. The physician may need to indicate that a basic procedure or service performed by another physician had to be repeated.

**78** Revised for 2008. Unplanned return to the operating or procedure room by the same physician following initial procedure for a related procedure during the postoperative period. This modifier indicates that complications arose to necessitate a return trip to the OR. The reimbursement is limited to the intraoperative percentage only. An OR is defined as a place of surface specifically equipped and staffed for the sole purpose of performing procedures. The term includes a cardiac catheterization suite, a laser suite, or an endoscopy suite. It does not include a patient's room, a minor treatment room, a recovery room, or an intensive care unit.

**79** Unrelated procedure or service by the same physician during the postoperative period. This modifier indicates that there was a procedure done during the global period that was not related to any postoperative complication. Although unrelated to the surgery, it may still be related to the disease process. It is not a staged procedure.

**GA** Identifies a service for which an advance beneficiary notice (ABN) has been completed and signed by the patient.

## Ambulatory Surgery Center Modifiers

**73** Discontinued outpatient/ASC procedure prior to administration of anesthesia. Due to extenuating circumstances that threaten the well-being of the patient, the physician may cancel a procedure subsequent to the patient's surgical preparation, including sedation when provided, and being taken to the operating suite but prior to the administration of local, regional, or general anesthesia. Under these circumstances, the intended service that is prepared for but cancelled can be reported by its usual procedure number and the addition of modifier 73. For physician reporting of a discontinued procedure, see modifier 53.

**74** Discontinued outpatient/ASC procedure after administration of anesthesia. Due to extenuating circumstances that threaten the well-being of the patient, the physician may terminate a procedure after the administration of local, regional, or general anesthesia or after the procedure was started. Under these circumstances, the procedure started but terminated can be reported by its usual procedure number and the addition of modifier 74. For physician reporting of a discontinued procedure, see modifier 53.

**SG** Identifies the facility portion of a service. Eliminated for Medicare claims effective January 1, 2008.

chapter 9

# Review Questions

## Using Modifiers Effectively

*Identify the letter of the choice that best completes the statement or answers the question.*

_____ 1. Modifiers are used for the following reasons:
- a. To alter or change the meaning of the assigned code.
- b. To decrease reimbursement.
- c. To increase reimbursement.
- d. All of the above.

_____ 2. When billing an endoscopy and a separately identifiable E/M service on the same day, the correct modifier is:
- a. 57
- b. 59
- c. 24
- d. 25

*Match the modifier description with the correct CPT modifier. (Use CPT manual, Appendix A.)*

a. Reference (outside) laboratory
b. Surgical care only
c. Postoperative management only
d. Mandated service
e. Assistant surgeon
f. Assistant surgeon (when qualified resident surgeon is not available)
g. Unusual anesthesia
h. Significant, separately identifiable evaluation and management service by the same physician on the same day of the procedure or other service
i. Professional component
j. Anesthesia by surgeon
k. Prolonged evaluation and management service
l. Unrelated evaluation and management service by the same physician during a postoperative period
m. Bilateral procedure
n. Discontinued procedure

_____ 3. 21 _____ 4. 23 _____ 5. 24
_____ 6. 25 _____ 7. 26 _____ 8. 32
_____ 9. 47 _____ 10. 50 _____ 11. 53
_____ 12. 54 _____ 13. 55 _____ 14. 80
_____ 15. 82 _____ 16. 90

chapter 10

# HCPCS Coding

Healthcare Common Procedure Coding System (HCPCS), created by the Health Care Financing Administration (HCFA), now the Centers for Medicare and Medicaid Services (CMS), is a uniform method for health care providers and medical suppliers to report professional services, procedures, and supplies. It is used primarily for Medicare billing, but many private payers recognize HCPCS codes. HCPCS Level I codes are the same as CPT codes.

## I. HCPCS Level II Codes Overview

- CPT does not contain all the codes needed to report medical services and supplies.
- Level II codes consist of one alpha character (A–V) followed by four digits.
- They are grouped by type of service or supply they represent.
- Level II also contains modifiers that are alphanumeric or two letters in the range from AA to VP.

## II. HCPCS Alphanumeric Codes

**A Codes** Transportation services including ambulance; medical and surgical supplies; administrative, miscellaneous, and investigational services.

**B Codes** Enteral and parenteral nutrition. A Certification of Medical Necessity (CMN) is required for coverage. Submit a revision to the CMN if the patient's daily volume changes by more than one (1) liter, if there is a change in infusion method, or if there is a change from premix to home mix or from parenteral to enteral therapy.

**C Codes** Temporary codes for use with Outpatient Prospective Payment System.

**D Codes** Dental procedures.

**E Codes** Durable Medical Equipment (DME). Before an item can be considered to be DME, it must meet all the following requirements:

- It must be able to withstand repeated use.

- It must be primarily and customarily used to serve a medical purpose.
- It is generally not useful to a person in the absence of an illness or injury.
- Appropriate for use in the home.

*NOTE: Do not confuse HCPCS "E" codes used for DME with the ICD-9-CM "E" codes used for coding diagnoses for external causes. There is no connection between HCPCS codes and ICD-9-CM Alpha Codes.*

**G Codes** Temporary procedures/professional services. Usually assigned to procedures and services that are being reviewed prior to inclusion in the CPT manual or screening procedures mandated by Congress. Once CPT assigns a code for these services, the G codes are usually removed.

**H Codes** Alcohol and drug abuse treatment services.

**J Codes** Drugs administered other than orally and chemotherapy drugs.

**K Codes** Temporary, assigned to DME regional carriers (DMERC).

**L Codes** Orthotic procedures; prosthetic procedures.

**M Codes** Other medical services.

**P Codes** Pathology and laboratory services.

**Q Codes** Temporary codes. When permanent code is assigned, the Q code is deleted.

**R Codes** Diagnostic radiology services; transportation.

**S Codes** Temporary national codes for private insurers other than Medicare.

**V Codes** Vision services; hearing services.

*NOTE: Do not confuse HCPCS "V" codes used for vision and hearing services with the ICD-9-CM diagnostic "V" codes used for classifying factors that influence health status.*

# III. HCPCS Symbols and Abbreviations

HCPCS uses the CPT book conventions to indicate new, revised, and deleted codes:

- A black circle (●) precedes a new code.
- A black triangle (▲) precedes a code with revised terminology or rules.
- Codes deleted from the active codes appear with a ~~strikeout~~.

A few of the subsections, headings, or codes have special instructions that apply only to that section. The term "NOTE" sometimes, but not always, is used to identify such instructions.

- Age and sex edits:
  P: Pediatric; years 0–10
  A: Adult; years 11–99
  M: Maternity; years 12–50
  S: Senior; years 50–99

- Gender is indicated by the icons:
  ♀ for female
  ♂ for male

Coverage issues associated with certain codes can be found in the Medicare Coverage Issue Manual (CIM) and Medicare Carriers Manual (MCM) and are usually included as an appendix in the HCPCS book and referenced if identified by a specific code.

# IV. Selecting a HCPCS Code

To locate a HCPCS Level II code, follow these steps:

1. Identify the services or procedures the patient received.
   Example: Screening flexible sigmoidoscopy.
2. Look up the appropriate term in the index.
   Example: Sigmoidoscopy.
3. Assign a tentative code.
   Example: Code G0104 or G0106 is tentatively assigned.
   Coding Tip: To the right of the terminology you may find a single code or multiple codes, a cross-reference, or an indication that the code has been deleted. Tentatively assign all codes listed.
4. Locate the code in the appropriate section.
   Example: G0104 Colorectal cancer screening; flexible sigmoidoscopy.
5. Check for color bars, symbols, notes, and references. Color bar means special coverage instructions apply. Review the appendixes for the reference definitions and other guidelines for coverage issues that apply.
6. Determine whether any modifiers should be used.
7. Assign the code.
   Example: The code assigned is G0104.

# V. HCPCS Coding Standards

- When both the CPT and HCPCS Level II code have virtually identical narratives for a procedure or service, the CPT code should be used, unless instructed by Medicare to use the HCPCS code.
- If the narratives are not identical (CPT code narrative is generic and HCPCS code is specific) the Level II HCPCS code should be used.
- Be sure to check for a HCPCS code when a CPT code description instructs you to include additional information, such as describing a specific medication.
- Submit a special report with the claim when a new, unusual, or variable procedure is provided or a modifier is used. Include the following information:
  - A copy of the appropriate report (e.g., operative, X-ray), explaining the nature, extent, and need for the procedure.
  - Documentation of the medical necessity for the procedure.
  - Documentation of the additional time and effort necessary to perform the procedure.

chapter 10

# Review Questions

## HCPCS Coding

*Indicate whether the sentence or statement is true or false.*

T F 1. "Hickpicks" is the correct pronunciation of the acronym HCPCS.

*Identify the letter of the choice that best completes the statement or answers the question.*

2. HCPCS is a coding system unlike ICD-9-CM or CPT. How many levels are found in the system?
   a. Five
   b. Two
   c. Ten
   d. Three

3. When billing Medicare, which code for screening colonoscopy would you use for a patient who has a grandfather with colon cancer?
   a. G0105
   b. G0104
   c. 45378
   d. G0121

4. HCPCS provides specific codes for equipment, services, procedures, supplies, injectables, prosthetics, and orthotics. CPT offers only one code for supplies. This code is:
   a. 99580
   b. 99366
   c. 99909
   d. 99070

5. J codes represent drugs and injectables in the HCPCS system. Several unique characteristics are inherent in this HCPCS section. Choose the correct attributes.
   a. Dosage, route of administration, generic name
   b. Product name, route of administration, cost
   c. Average wholesale price, product name, dosage
   d. None of the above

6. HCPCS modifiers are presented in what format?
   a. Two numeric digits
   b. Alphanumeric characters
   c. Alphabetic or numeric characters
   d. Alphabetic characters

***Complete each sentence or statement.***

7. Level II HCPCS codes are sometimes referred to as ________________________ codes.

8. HCPCS Code S2083 "Adjustment of gastric band diameter via subcutaneous port by injection or aspiration of saline" is considered a ____________________code.

9. Several code series in HCPCS contain temporary codes. Those codes are in the following series: ________________________, ________________________, and ________________________.

10. When the CPT code is general and the HCPCS National Code is more specific, use the ________________________ code.

chapter 11

# ICD-9-CM Conventions and Rules

## I. Importance of Accurate ICD-9-CM Coding

- ICD-9-CM codes provide clearly defined diagnoses, signs, or symptoms that allow efficient claim processing.
- An error in diagnosis coding conveys the wrong reason a patient received medical services and may lead to a denial because of medical necessity.
- The primary diagnosis is why the patient came to the office (chief complaint). It is considered the patient's major health problem and is listed first.
- A concurrent condition is a disorder that coexists with the primary condition that complicates the treatment of the primary condition and should be coded after the primary diagnosis.
- A secondary diagnosis is a disorder running concurrently with the primary diagnosis but does not overtly affect the prognosis of the primary condition.
- Concurrent and secondary conditions are assigned to the second through the fourth diagnosis positions.

Example: A patient arrives at the office with a complaint of lower right quadrant abdominal pain. While the patient is at the office, the physician also reviews the current status and treatment of the patient's diabetes and essential hypertension. The diagnosis (Dx) should be listed as follows:

- Primary Dx: Lower right abdominal pain
- Concurrent Dx: Diabetes mellitus
- Secondary Dx: Essential hypertension

## II. The ICD-9-CM Book

Volume 1 Tabular list, with five appendixes that provide more detailed information about the patient's clinical condition:

- Morphology of Neoplasms
- Glossary of Mental Disorders

- Classification of Drugs
- Classification of Industrial Accidents
- List of Three-Digit Categories

Volume 2 Alphabetic index; contains three sections.

Volume 3 Procedure codes used for hospital billing only.

*NOTE: Although the tabular list is labeled Volume 1 and the alphabetic list is labeled Volume 2, the alphabetic list appears first in many ICD-9-CM manuals. Therefore, this manual addresses each section in the order of appearance. To code accurately, you should be familiar with the structure of the ICD-9-CM manual and read the Introduction and Coding Guidelines provided at the beginning of the text.*

# III. Alphabetic Index

Section 1 is the index of diseases and injuries. This section also contains special tables for indexing codes for hypertension and neoplasms (tumors).

Section 2 is the table of drugs and chemicals in alphabetic order with corresponding codes related to poisonings.

Section 3 is the alphabetic index of all external causes of injuries and poisonings, not just those resulting from drugs or chemicals.

The most important ICD-9-CM conventions in the alphabetic index are:

- Main term, which appears in bold-faced type according to condition.
- Modifiers, which help define the main term but have no effect on the selection of code.
- Subterm, which is indented underneath the main term in regular type. The subterm may describe essential differences in body site, etiology (the cause of the disease), or clinical type.
- Cross-reference, which indicates where to look for additional modifiers, anatomical sites, or main terms.

# IV. Tabular List

The tabular list presents diagnostic codes in numerical order. V codes and E codes are found as supplementary classifications at the end of the tabular list.

## A. V Codes

V codes classify factors that influence health status or give reasons why when there is no clear Dx or disease.

- V codes are used when there are factors influencing health status or there are valid medical reasons for contacting a health facility but a definitive Dx or active symptoms cannot be, or have not been, stated.
- It is appropriate to use V codes when the following occur:
  - When a patient is not sick but receives a service for a purpose, such as a screening colonoscopy.

- When a patient with a current or recurring condition receives treatment, such as physical therapy.
- When a patient has a past condition that affects current health status or has a family history of disease.

- Examples:
  - Family history of colon cancer
  - Routine follow-up
  - Screening for malignant neoplasm of the colon
  - Yearly physical
  - Routine follow-up for possible recurrence of tumor

## B. E Codes

E codes are diagnostic codes for external causes of poisoning or injuries.

- These codes describe the external cause of an injury, poisoning, or adverse reaction affecting the patient's health.
- E codes are used in addition to the main code.
- E codes are primarily required for Worker's Compensation and liability insurance.
- They are used to define what happened and where it happened.
- Some E codes should be considered very carefully before they are used because of their sensitive nature. For instance, suicide attempts and assaults may be highly confidential.

## C. Appendix A

Appendix A lists M codes that identify the morphology of neoplasms. These:

- Indicate whether a tumor is benign or malignant.
- Are used for statistical purposes in hospital reports rather than on insurance claim forms.
- Are not used by physicians.

# V. Additional ICD-9-CM Conventions

### *Conventions*

**NOS** Not otherwise specified; code should be avoided, if possible.

**NEC** Not elsewhere classified; should not be used as a shortcut to avoid looking up a more specific code. The abbreviation indicates that the condition requiring the code assignment is vague. Get further information from the patient record or from staff.

[ ] Brackets; used around synonyms, alternative wordings, or explanations of codes that appear in slanted brackets. These codes should only be used as secondary codes and only if supported by physician documentation.

( ) Parentheses; used around descriptions that do not affect the code (nonessential modifiers).

: Colon; used in the tabular list after an incomplete term that needs one of the modifiers that follow to make it assignable.

{ } Braces; enclose a series of terms, each of which is modified by the statement that appears to the right of the brace.

### *Cross-References*

| | |
|---|---|
| **See** | Appears when an anatomical site is used as the main condition. |
| **See Also** | Requires looking for a second main term before deciding on the code. |
| **See Condition** | Indicates that you have focused on the wrong word in the diagnostic statement and directs investigation of special conditions that appear in the tabular list after the specified code number. |

## VI. General Rules for Diagnostic Coding

- Never begin searching in the tabular list (Volume 1). It is too easy to misidentify a diagnosis and code incorrectly.
- As a general rule, never code from Volume 2 (alphabetic index). Exceptions are the neoplasm and hypertension tables. After finding the code in Volume 2, go to the tabular list to obtain the code with the highest level of specificity.
- All physician claims must contain valid ICD-9-CM diagnostic codes.
- When coding "circumstances" in lieu of actual disease or illness, use the V codes.
- Diagnostic codes should be sequenced with the primary diagnosis first. Then code the secondary or coexisting conditions.
- Look for the condition, not the site.
- Check all indentions to ensure you have coded the most appropriate code.
- Do not code a diagnosis for a condition a patient no longer has unless it has a significant importance relative to the claim being billed.
- Do not code a rule out or suspected diagnosis or one that is possible or probable. Code based on the patient's symptoms or condition until test results indicate a confirmed diagnosis.
- Always carry the ICD-9-CM code to the highest level of specificity. Only a limited number of diagnostic codes are three digit codes. If there is a fourth digit, it must be used. If there is a fifth digit, it must be used.
- It is acceptable to repeatedly use a chronic diagnosis as often as necessary as long as the patient is not symptomatic. Do not add diagnoses for the purpose of giving variety to the patient's condition.
- For a surgical procedure, code the diagnosis for which the procedure is being performed, only if no abnormality is identified.

## VII. Signs and Symptoms Rules

Signs and symptoms should be used when:

- The patient has a symptomatic, chronic condition and is experiencing a flare-up and/or exacerbation. The chronic condition should be the secondary diagnosis.

- A principal diagnosis has not been established at the conclusion of the visit or encounter.
- No more specific diagnosis for the condition can be made at the end of the encounter/visit.
- Presenting signs/symptoms are transient, and no definitive diagnosis is made.
- The symptom is treated in an outpatient setting, and no additional work-up is necessary to arrive at a more definitive diagnosis.

# VIII. Table of Drugs and Chemicals

- Determine whether the patient's problem is poisoning or an adverse effect. Remember that poisoning means wrong drug/substance or incorrect dosage.
- Identify the chemical substance, and locate the correct choice.
- Obtain appropriate code number.
- Assign the secondary code for the effects.
- Use an E code to reflect external cause.

# IX. Guidelines for Coding Trauma/Injuries

- Primary axis indicates the type of injury (e.g., fracture).
- Injuries classifiable to more than one subcategory should be coded separately unless a combination code is available.
- Always code the most severe injury as the primary diagnosis.
- Late effect injury codes are always coded after the residual condition.
- Assign V codes for aftercare required for wires, pins, plates, and external fixation devices.
- Assign E codes for accidents.

# X. Summary for Using ICD-9-CM Codes

- An ICD-9-CM code should be selected to describe the diagnosis, symptom, complaint, condition, or problem for which the service was performed.
- The primary diagnosis should be coded first, followed by a secondary diagnosis. Coexisting conditions pertaining to the treatment given should also be coded.
- Code to the highest degree of specificity. Some ICD-9-CM codes require additional fourth or fifth digits.
- Chronic conditions treated on an ongoing basis may be coded as many times as required for treatment and care of the patient or when applicable to the patient's care plan.
- List the appropriate V code first and the problem second when only ancillary services are provided.
  Example: If a patient is receiving only ancillary therapeutic services (physical therapy), use the V code first, followed by the code for the condition. However, if the surgeon or primary doctor is seeing that patient for another reason, the numerical code is listed first and the V code is listed as a subsequent code.

- Do not code diagnosis as "probable," "suspected," "questionable," or "rule out." Instead, code the signs, symptoms, and abnormal test result(s) or other reason for the visit.
- Do not code conditions previously treated or those that no longer exist, although a V code for history of previous conditions could be coded, if appropriate.
- Each medical service and surgical procedure should be assigned a corresponding diagnostic code.
- When physicians report diagnostic services on a claim form, payers look for a direct relationship between the diagnostic services and the ICD-9-CM codes submitted.
- For surgical procedures, code the diagnosis applicable to the procedure. If the postoperative diagnosis is different from the preoperative diagnosis, use the postoperative diagnosis code.
- Code "reason for the visit" first, not necessarily the most serious condition the patient may have. When a diagnosis or impression is not available, the chief complaint can provide symptoms for use to support/report the service rendered. List additional codes to describe any coexisting conditions managed by the physician that day.

# Gastroenterology ICD-9-CM Signs and Symptom Codes (Updated for 2008)

| | | | |
|---|---|---|---|
| 276.50 | Volume depletion, unspecified | 783.7 | Failure to thrive, adult |
| 276.51 | Dehydration | 783.41 | Failure to thrive, pediatric |
| 276.52 | Hypovolemia | 785.0 | Tachycardia |
| 278.02 | Overweight | 785.6 | Lymphadenopathy |
| 564.4 | Diarrhea following GI surgery | 786.09 | Respiratory distress |
| 564.5 | Functional diarrhea | 787.01 | Nausea and vomiting |
| 567.21 | Generalized peritonitis | 787.02 | Nausea alone |
| 567.22 | Peritoneal abscess | 787.03 | Vomiting alone |
| 567.23 | Spontaneous bacterial peritonitis | 787.1 | Heartburn |
| 567.29 | Other suppurative peritonitis | 787.20 | Dysphagia, unspecified |
| 567.38 | Other retroperitoneal abscess | 787.21 | Dysphagia, oral phase |
| 567.39 | Other retroperitoneal infections | 787.22 | Dysphagia, oropharyngeal phase |
| 567.81 | Choleperitonitis | 787.23 | Dysphagia, pharyngeal phase |
| 567.82 | Sclerosing mesenteritis | 787.24 | Dysphagia, pharyngoesophageal phase |
| 567.89 | Other specified peritonitis | 787.29 | Other dysphagia |
| 585.1 | Chronic kidney disease, stage I | 787.6 | Incontinence, feces |
| 585.2 | Chronic kidney disease, state II (mild) | 787.7 | Abnormal feces |
| 585.3 | Chronic kidney disease, stage III (moderate) | 787.91 | Diarrhea |
| 585.4 | Chronic kidney disease, stage IV (severe) | 787.99 | Change in bowel habits |
| 585.5 | Chronic kidney disease, stage V | 789.01 | RUQ pain |
| 585.6 | End stage kidney disease | 789.02 | LUQ pain |
| 585.9 | Chronic kidney disease, unspecified | 789.03 | RLQ pain |
| 780.6 | Fever | 789.04 | LLQ pain |
| 780.94 | Early satiety | 789.05 | Periumbilic pain |
| 780.99 | Other general symptoms | 789.06 | Epigastric pain |
| 782.4 | Jaundice, unspecified | 789.07 | Generalized abdominal pain |
| 783.0 | Anorexia | 789.09 | Other specified abdominal pain or multiple sites |
| 783.0 | Loss of appetite | 789.1 | Hepatomegaly |
| 783.1 | Abnormal weight gain | 789.2 | Splenomegaly |
| 783.21 | Abnormal weight loss | 789.51 | Ascites, malignant |
| 783.22 | Underweight | 789.59 | Ascites, other |
| 783.3 | Feeding difficulties | 789.5 | Ascites |

*(continued)*

| | | | |
|---|---|---|---|
| 789.9 | Umbilical discharge | 794.5 | Abnormal thyroid scan |
| 789.51 | Malignant ascites | 794.8 | Abnormal liver scan |
| 789.59 | Other ascites | 794.9 | Abnormal CCK-HIDA or pancreas scan |
| 790.01 | Abnormal drop in hematocrit | 796.2 | Elevated blood pressure |
| 790.4 | Abnormal liver enzymes | 796.3 | Low blood pressure |
| 790.5 | Abnormal amylase | 799.01 | Asphyxia |
| 790.92 | Abnormal protime | 799.02 | Hypoxemia |
| 792.1 | Abnormal stool contents | 799.2 | Nerves/nervousness |
| 793.3 | Abnormal biliary study | 799.3 | Debility |
| 793.4 | Abnormal GI study | 799.4 | Cachexia |
| 793.6 | Abnormal abdominal study | | |

chapter 11

# Review Questions

## ICD-9-CM Conventions and Rules

***Indicate whether the sentence or statement is true or false.***

T F 1. Some ICD-9-CM codes do not require a fifth digit, but all diagnosis codes must have at least four digits.

T F 2. NEC is an abbreviation for "no entry classified."

T F 3. The V code supplement to the ICD-9-CM system describes external causes of injury.

T F 4. Subterms are also known as essential modifiers.

***Identify the letter of the choice that best completes the statement or answers the question.***

5. The official version of ICD-9-CM for physician's services is organized into two volumes titled:
   a. Tabular List Index and Procedure Tabular List
   b. Index and Procedure Tabular List and Alphabetic Index
   c. Tabular List of Diseases and Alphabetical Index of Diseases
   d. Numerical Alphabet and Procedure Tabular, and Alphabetic List

6. Supplemental listings follow the 17 numeric chapters of Volume 1 of ICD-9-CM, which are:
   a. Alphanumeric codes and tables
   b. Alphanumeric V and E codes
   c. Numeric V and E codes
   d. Table of drugs, chemicals, and neoplasms

7. The principal diagnosis is:
   a. The diagnosis, after study, determined to be the reason the patient sought medical care.
   b. The first diagnosis on the physician office CMS 1500 form.
   c. The most important diagnosis that is also the most serious diagnosis that affects the patient's potential for wellness.
   d. The diagnosis, after study, that was the major cause for hospital admission.

***Complete each sentence or statement.***

8. The ICD-9-CM system is used to translate ____________________ information into numeric codes.

9. NEC stands for ________________________________ when used with ill-defined terms to advise the coder that specified forms of the condition are classified differently.

10. The term __________________ directs coder to use Volume 1, Tabular List, for additional information.

chapter 12

# Abstracting and Coding Operative Reports

## I. The Process

- Read the entire documentation for the service to obtain an overview of the problems presented and procedures/services performed. Research any word or abbreviation not understood.
- Reread the problem and highlight the diagnosis, symptoms, or health status that supports, justifies, and/or proves the medical necessity of any procedure or service performed.
  - Make a copy of the original document for markup purposes, and then shred after the abstracting and coding process has been completed.
  - Do not use highlighter or other marker on an original document.
- List and code the documented procedure(s) or service(s) performed.
- Assign required modifiers, if applicable.
- List the diagnosis(es), symptoms, or reasons the patient sought health care that justify performing the procedure.
- Identify the primary condition.
- Code the diagnosis(es) or symptoms listed.
- Link each procedure or service to a diagnosis, symptom, or health status to communicate the documented medical necessity for performing the procedure.

## II. Procedure for Coding Operative Reports

1. Make a copy of the report.
2. Carefully review the listing of procedures performed (located in the outline section of the report).
3. Read the body of the report and make a note of the procedures you would expect to code. Key words to look for include the following:
   - Simple versus complicated
   - Partial, complete, total, or incomplete

- Unilateral versus bilateral
- Initial versus subsequent
- Incision versus excision
- Endoscopy
- Biopsy
- Ligation
- Debridement
- Complex, simple, intermediate, repair
- Reconstruction
- Diagnostic versus surgical procedure
- Screening

4. Be alert to the following situations:
   - Additional procedures documented in the body of the report but not listed in the "operative procedure" or "procedure performed" section of the report. Example: The "procedure performed" may state that polyps were removed using one method but the body of the report identifies two distinct methods of removal.
   - The procedure performed section lists procedures performed but the procedure is not described in the body of the operative report. In these cases, the physician will have to add a written addendum to the procedure report documenting the performance of any listed procedure that should be coded. Example: The "procedure performed" states that the esophagus was dilated, but there is no mention of the dilation in the body of the report.
5. Identify main term(s) and subterms for the procedure(s) to be coded.
6. Underline and research any terms in the report that you cannot define. Many major coding errors are made when the coder does not understand critical medical terms in the report.
7. Locate the main term(s) in the CPT index. Check for the proper anatomic site or organ.
8. Research all suggested codes. Read all notes and guidelines pertaining to the codes you are investigating. Watch for "add-on" procedures described in any notes/guidelines.
9. Return to the index and research additional codes if you cannot find a particular code(s) that matches the description of the procedure(s) performed in the operative report.

   *NOTE: Because there is a monetary value for each CPT code, never use multiple, separate codes to describe a procedure if the CPT has a single code that includes all of the individual components of the procedure described by the physician.*

   *NOTE: Never use a code described in CPT as a "separate procedure" when it is performed with other procedures within the same family of codes as the primary procedure, as it is considered an integral part of the greater procedure.*
10. Investigate the possibility of adding modifiers to a specific code description to fully explain the procedure(s) performed.

    Example: Key word indicators for use of modifier 22 include the following:
    - Excessive bleeding (>500 cc)
    - Friable tissue
    - Prolonged procedure due to ____________
    - Unusual anatomy, findings, or circumstances
    - Very difficult
    - More than ten polyps removed or biopsies performed

11. Code the postoperative diagnosis first. This should explain the medical necessity for performing the procedure(s). If the postoperative diagnosis does not support the procedure performed, be sure the patient's chart contains documentation to justify the procedure.
    Example: Patient referred to the practice to evaluate GI bleed. A colonoscopy is performed with no abnormalities found. The diagnosis that should be billed for the colonoscopy is GI bleed.
    *NOTE: Look for additional findings in the body of the report if the postoperative diagnosis listed on the operative report does not completely justify the medical necessity for the procedure. Compare the post-operative diagnosis with the biopsy report on all excised neoplasms to determine whether the tissue is benign or malignant. Do not code an excision until the pathology report is received.*
12. Review code options with the physician who performed the procedure if the case is unusual. Before assigning an "unlisted CPT procedure" code, check HCPCS level II and III codes. Remember that a description of the procedure performed must accompany the claim form if an unlisted CPT code is reported.
13. Assign final codes for procedures verified in steps 3 and 4 and any addendum the physician added to the original report.
14. Properly sequence the codes listing the most significant procedure performed during the episode first. Be sure to destroy the copy of the operative report (i.e., shred it) after the abstracting and coding process is complete.

chapter 12

# Review Questions

## Abstracting and Coding Operative Reports

***Identify the letter of the choice that best completes the statement or answers the question.***

1. When reviewing an operative report and discovering that there was excessive bleeding greater than 500 cc, you should evaluate using:
   a. An adjunct diagnosis
   b. Modifier 22
   c. Modifier 59
   d. An adjunct procedure

2. Coding an excision in which tissue was sent to pathology requires:
   a. Coding the pathology service with the excision procedure.
   b. Coding the excision as "undetermined" pathology to avoid deferring workload.
   c. Deferring coding until the pathology report is received.
   d. Coding the excision using the worst case plausible.

3. When abstracting clinical scenarios prior to coding, make a copy of the original document and ____________________ the copy when abstracting and coding is completed.
   a. File with the explanation of benefits.
   b. File by date of service.
   c. File in the shredding machine.
   d. File with the patient's medical record.

4. Each procedure or service should be linked to a diagnosis in order to:
   a. Inform the patient of their poor health.
   b. Document medical necessity.
   c. Determine physician competence.
   d. Assist in developing a prognosis.

5. When abstracting an operative report, the coder discovers that the "procedures performed" section lists a procedure that is not described in the body of the operative report. The coder should:
   a. Not code the procedure; if it was not documented, it was not done.
   b. Destroy the operative report and have the surgeon dictate a new one.
   c. Code the procedure, making a note on the operative report that the procedure was done.
   d. Request the physician add an addendum to the operative report.

6. Justification for performing a procedure is best supported by:
    a. Emergency room signs and symptoms.
    b. Primary diagnosis.
    c. Family history.
    d. Postoperative diagnosis.

7. In abstracting a procedure report in which several procedures were performed:
    a. Code only the first three procedures.
    b. Code the highest valued procedure first.
    c. Code all of the procedures in numerical order.
    d. Code in the order they were performed.

***Identify the letter of the choice that does not apply.***

8. When reporting an "unlisted" CPT procedure, a description of the procedure must:
    a. Accompany the claim form.
    b. Be submitted by fax for electronic claims.
    c. Be on file until the explanation of benefits is received.
    d. Justify the medical necessity for the procedure.

chapter 13

# Anatomy and Medical Terminology

Medical terminology is used to describe diagnoses and procedures. Medical terms can be broken down into the following four parts:

- Root: The basic, or core, part of a term that means something. Roots usually come from Greek or Latin. They often mean a body part.
  Example: colon
- Prefix: One or more letters placed before the root to change its meaning.
  Example: "Bi" is a prefix that means two or twice. When bi is at the beginning of the word lateral to form bilateral, the meaning is "having two sides."
- Suffix: One or more letters placed after the root to change its meaning.
  Examples: "Itis" means inflammation, indicating damaged tissue that is red/painful. The word diverticulitis means inflammation of the diverticula. "Ectomy" means removal. Polypectomy means removal of a polyp.
- Combining vowel: A letter used for connecting roots with other word parts. The vowel is usually an "o," but sometimes it is an "a" or "i." When a combining vowel is added to a root the result is called a *combining form.*

| Parts of the body | Combining form | Parts of the body | Combining form |
|---|---|---|---|
| Artery | Arteri(o) | Digestive system | Gastr(o) |
| Blood | Hemat(o) | Liver | Hepat(o) |
| Bone | Oste(o) | Lung | Pneum(o) |
| Chest | Thorac(o) | Mouth | Stomat(o) |
| Head | Cephal(o) | Skin | Dermat(o) |
| Heart | Cardi(o),(a) | Vein | Phleb(o) |

Medical terminology is based on anatomy, the study of the body's structure.

- The basic structural unit of the body is the cell.
- Groups of cells combine to form tissue.
- Related tissues join to form an organ.
- Each organ works with others in a body system.

# I. Digestive System

The digestive system includes the mouth, pharynx, esophagus, stomach, small intestine, large intestine, liver, gallbladder, and pancreas. The digestive system carries out five important functions:

- Breaking up food into smaller pieces (mouth).
- Transporting food through the digestive tract by means of muscle contractions (pharynx to the stomach).
- Producing enzymes that speed up chemical changes in food; the stomach produces gastric juice.
- Absorbing nutrients into the bloodstream; the small intestine uses digestive juices from the liver, gallbladder, and pancreas to complete the breakdown.
- Getting rid of solid wastes (colon or large intestine); wastes leave the body through the anus at the end of the rectum.

The esophagus is a tube through which food passes from the pharynx to the stomach. The junction between the esophagus and the stomach (the gastroesophageal junction or GE junction) is not actually considered a valve, although it is sometimes called the cardiac valve.

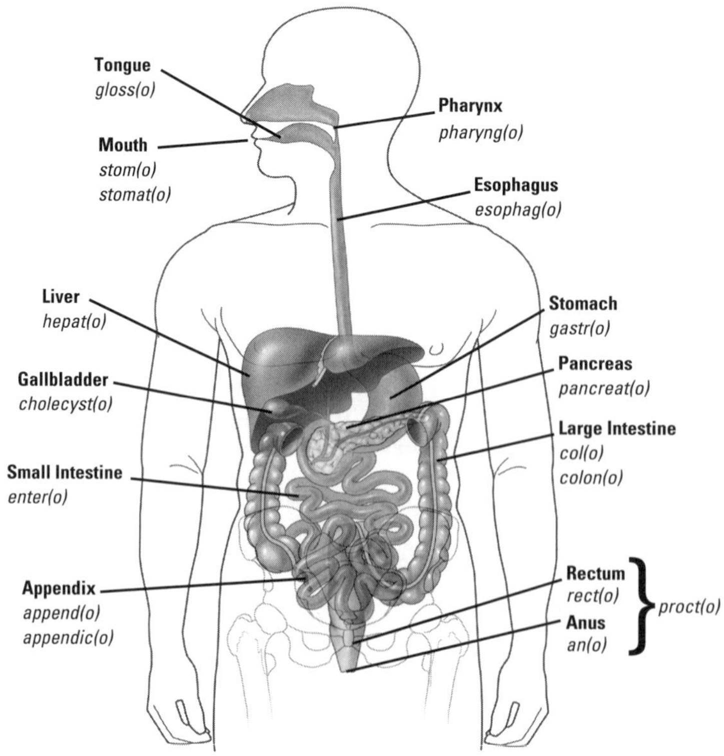

The stomach is divided into four sections, each of which has different cells and functions. The cardia is where the contents of the esophagus empty into the stomach. The fundus is formed by the upper curvature of the stomach. The body or corpus is the main, central region. The pylorus or antrum is the lower section of the stomach that facilitates emptying contents into the small intestine. Two smooth muscle valves, or sphincters, keep the contents of the stomach contained. They are the cardiac or esophageal sphincter dividing the tract above, and the pyloric sphincter dividing the stomach from the small intestine.

The pancreas is located posterior to the stomach and in close association with the duodenum. It is often described as having three regions: a head, body and tail. The pancreatic head abuts the second part of the duodenum. The body of the pancreas lies at the level of L2 on the spine. The tail of the pancreas extends toward the spleen.

The small intestine has three structural parts: duodenum, the first and shortest part is 25 cm (9.84 in) in length; jejunum, which is the central portion and 2.5 m (8.2 ft) in length; and ileum is 3.5 m (11.5 ft) in length and separated from the cecum by the ileocecal valve.

The large instestine, or colon, is the last part of the digestive system. It has the following anatomic parts and features:

- Cecum, the first part of the large intestine
- Vermiform appendix, a small appendage on the cecum containing lymphatic tissue
- Ascending colon
- Right colic (hepatic) flexure
- Transverse colon
- Left colic (splenic) flexure
- Descending colon
- Sigmoid colon, the s-shaped region of the large intestine
- Rectosigmoid colon
- Rectum
- Anal canal, the last segment of the large intestine
- Anus

## II. Terminology

| Suffix | Meaning | Term | Meaning |
|---|---|---|---|
| -emesis<br>Hemat(o)- | Vomiting<br>Blood | Hematemesis | Vomiting of blood |
| -iasis<br>Lith(o)- | Diseased condition<br>Stone | Cholelithiasis | Stone in the gallbladder (gallstone) |
| -ostomy | An opening | Colostomy | Surgical creation of an opening between the colon and the outside of the body, forming an artificial anus |
| -phagia | Eating and swallowing | Dysphagia | Difficulty swallowing |
| | | Colitis | Inflammation of the colon |
| | | Appendectomy | Surgical removal of the appendix |
| | | Gastrorrhea | Excessive secretion of mucus or gastric juices in the stomach |

chapter 13

# Review Questions

## Anatomy and Medical Terminology

***Identify the letter of the choice that best completes the statement or answers the question.***

1. The study of the body's structure is termed:
   a. Human species
   b. Physiology
   c. System of human development
   d. Anatomy

2. Muscles that work without a person's direction, such as respiration, are:
   a. Involuntary muscles
   b. Voluntary muscles, because they work voluntarily
   c. Striated muscles
   d. Contractile muscles

3. The largest organ of the body is the:
   a. Stomach
   b. Liver
   c. Lungs
   d. Skin

4. Absorbing nutrients into the bloodstream is a function performed by the:
   a. Circulatory system
   b. Integumentary system
   c. Digestive system
   d. Respiratory system

5. The digestive system does not include the following organ:
   a. Liver
   b. Kidney
   c. Pancreas
   d. Gallbladder

chapter 14

# Fraud and Abuse

## I. What Is Fraud?

Fraud is defined by the Office of the Inspector General (OIG) as

> Knowingly and willfully executing, or attempting to execute, a scheme or artifice to defraud any health care benefit program; or to obtain, by means of false or fraudulent pretenses, representations, or promises, any of the money or property owned by or under the custody or control of, any health care benefit program.

## II. Examples of Fraud

- Billing for services that were not rendered.
- Billing for services as your own when they were, in fact, performed by another entity not eligible to be paid by Medicare.
- Using an incorrect provider number in order to be paid, such as using a deceased physician's provider number in order to be paid.
- Signing blank records or certification forms that are used by another entity to obtain Medicare payment.
- Selling or sharing a patient's Medicare number for the purpose of filing false claims to Medicare.
- Soliciting, offering, or receiving a kickback, bribe, or rebate.
- Offering incentives to Medicare patients that are not offered to non-Medicare patients, such as routinely waiving or discounting the Medicare deductible and/or coinsurance amounts.
- Falsifying information on applications, medical records, billing statements, and/or cost reports or on any statement filed with the government.

- Misrepresenting as medically necessary noncovered screening services, such as diagnostic tests done as a part of a routine physical exam, by using inappropriate procedure or diagnosis codes.

## III. What Is Abuse?

According to the OIG,

> Abuse may, directly or indirectly, result in unnecessary costs to the Medicare/Medicaid program, improper payment, or payment for services that fail to meet professionally recognized standards of care, or that are medically unnecessary. Abuse involves payment for items or services when there is no legal entitlement to that payment and the provider has not knowingly and/or intentionally misrepresented facts to obtain payment.

## IV. Examples of Abuse

- Intentionally or unintentionally filing duplicate claims to the Medicare program, even if it does not result in duplicate payment.
- Using procedure/revenue codes that describe more extensive services than those actually performed.
- Collecting more than the 20% coinsurance or the deductible on claims filed to Medicare. Providers may, of course, bill the Medicare patient for services not covered (e.g., exclusions) by the Medicare program such as routine physical exams.
- Requiring a deposit or other payment (e.g., advance payment of deductible and/or coinsurance amounts) from a Medicare beneficiary as a condition for admission, continued care, or other provision of services.
- Billing for clinical laboratory tests that were, in fact, performed by another entity. The Medicare law precludes certain providers from billing for clinical tests performed, for example, by a clinical laboratory.
- Billing for services grossly in excess of those needed by the patient. For example, always billing for complete laboratory profiles when a single diagnostic test is needed to diagnose the patient's condition.

## V. Unacceptable Billing and Coding Practices

The most common fraudulent practices involve unbundling, upcoding, duplicate billing, overcharging, and unfair competitive practices. Specific examples include the following:

- A laboratory agrees to pay a physician for every patient referred for a specific study. This is a kickback situation that is prohibited by Federal law.
- A hospital, clinic, or independent laboratory unbundles a panel laboratory test to obtain a higher reimbursement.

- A physician bills Medicare for a noncovered service using a procedure code that is covered under the Medicare program.

## A. Upcoding

Upcoding involves claims submitted to any insurance company for services, supplies, or equipment that are reported with procedure or revenue codes that describe more extensive services/items than documented.

## B. Not Medically Necessary

- Services provided in a hospital or skilled nursing facility that, based on the condition of the patient, could have been provided elsewhere (such as the home or nursing home).
- E/M services provided in excess of what is considered medically reasonable and necessary.
- Therapy or diagnostic procedures provided in excess of medical need.

## C. Missed Appointments

CMS has a long-standing policy on the appropriate billing of patients for missed appointments. This policy allows physicians and suppliers to charge Medicare beneficiaries for missed appointments as long as non-Medicare and all other patients are also charged the same amount. The charge for a missed appointment is not a charge for a service itself but is considered a charge for a missed business opportunity. Therefore, if a physician's or supplier's missed appointment policy applies equally to all patients (Medicare and non-Medicare), then the Medicare law and regulations do not preclude the physician or supplier from charging the Medicare patient directly. To implement this policy, consider providing written notice to patients.

# VI. Appropriate Compliance Steps for the Physician

- Carefully document in the patient's file the medical necessity for all procedures.
- Do not order full blood test profiles when only one or two tests are necessary.
- If performing extraordinarily high numbers of particularly expensive procedures, be prepared to explain why this may be different than other physicians in the same specialty and geographic area.
- Review samples of Medicare claims on a monthly basis to ensure the accuracy of the listed procedure and diagnosis codes.
- Ensure there is no double billing of Medicare and private insurers for the same services.
- Properly train all employees who handle billing.
- Address employee concerns regarding inappropriate billing.
- Try to have employees leave on good terms.
- Document the reasons for any disciplinary actions taken against an employee.
- Do not make statements that are likely to be misconstrued if repeated to investigators.

- Be extremely careful about entering into lease space agreements with mobile providers. Be able to defend the payments as fair market value without any consideration of patient referrals, i.e., make sure the transaction would make economic sense if zero patients were referred to the mobile provider.

## VII. Antikickback and Stark Laws

It is important to consider whether any proposed activity appears in any way to provide to any referral source something of value that could be considered an inducement for patient referrals. Do not do the following:

- Pay for patient referrals in any manner.
- Provide free or improperly discounted equipment or services to any patient or referral source.
- Give gifts to any referral source, except for occasional nominal gifts for holidays, etc.
- Improperly enter into a lease with a referral source.
- Enter into any agreement for products or services with a referral source.

Remember to always review all documentation prior to signing.

chapter 14

# Review Questions

## Fraud and Abuse

***Indicate whether the sentence or statement is true or false.***

T F 1. Filing of duplicate claims to Medicare, even if it does not result in duplicate payment, can be considered abuse.

T F 2. If a laboratory agrees to pay a physician for every patient referred for a specific study, this is considered a kickback situation.

T F 3. Billing for services provided by another entity to obtain payment is a type of fraud.

T F 4. If a physician bills for a noncovered service using a procedure code that is covered, it is not considered fraud.

***Identify the letter of the choice that best completes the statement or answers the question.***

5. Examples of health care fraud include:
   a. Overutilization of health care services, billing for services not performed, and billing patients twice for the same service.
   b. Billing for services never performed.
   c. Overutilization of health care services and billing over the fee schedule amount.
   d. Overutilization of health care services.

6. Offices wishing to prevent fraudulent practices should:
   a. Never change or delete information stated in the medical record.
   b. Never add diagnoses to the claim form that have not been approved by medical personnel as appropriate to the patient's case.
   c. Never change or delete medical record information or add diagnoses to the claim form not approved by medical personnel.
   d. None of the above.

***Complete each sentence or statement.***

7. Upcoding is the ________________________ of an ICD-9-CM diagnosis code that does not match ____________________________________ for the purpose of illegally ________________________ reimbursement.

8. Self-referral involves providers ordering services to be performed for patients by organizations in which they have a ________________________ interest.

9. Unbundling is the reporting of ________________________ codes to increase reimbursement from a payer when a single ________________________ code should be reported.

10. One way to help the physician avoid fraud and abuse is to have a ________________________ in place in the office.

chapter 15

# HIPAA and Release of Information

## I. Legal and Regulatory Considerations

HIPAA is the acronym for the Health Insurance Portability and Accountability Act of 1996. The intent of the act is to combat waste and fraud and abuse in the health insurance and health care delivery systems, to protect the privacy of patient health information, and to allow employees to continue receiving health benefits when changing jobs.

The purpose of the privacy standard is to identify individual patient rights for the protection of health information by health care providers, health plans, and health care clearing houses. These entities are prohibited from using or disclosing protected health information (PHI) except as authorized by the patient or specifically permitted by HIPAA.

If the patient is unable to sign a release of information form, the form can be signed by:

- A parent or legal guardian for a minor child under 18 years of age.
- Person with power of attorney if patient is incompetent or incapacitated.

The medical office is required to comply with their state laws and regulations, if more restrictive than HIPAA, before releasing information from a patient's medical record.

## II. Confidentiality

The following are examples of breaches of confidentiality:

- Discussing the patient's health information over the phone with unauthorized individuals.
- Sending records to individuals without the patient's permission.
- Faxing medical records without a confidentiality cover.
- Communicating patient information to family members without the patient's consent.

To avoid breaches of confidentiality, always know the party you are talking to before providing information. In the case of a telephone conversation, it is prudent to obtain the caller's phone number and call them back so you know who or where the call initiated from.

Keep a log of the transmission of all medically sensitive faxes as well as copies of all receipt-of-transmittal verifications.

Faxed medical information should be limited to the information required to satisfy the immediate needs of the requesting party.

## III. Authorization to Release Medical Records

- Patients must sign an authorization to release records for any purpose other than treatment, payment, and health care operations.
- The authorization must include:
  - Who will be receiving the information
  - For what purpose it will be released
  - How long the release is good for; without a specific time frame, it is good for 1 year from the date signed

PHI may be released to the following without an authorization signed by the patient:

- To another health care professional treating the patient
- To the patient's health insurance company for payment
- To the patient
- *Subpoena duces tecum*
- Court order

The following records are exceptions that require specific authorization by the patient:

- Psychiatric and other sensitive confidential records
- HIV and AIDS records, sexually transmissible disease records, or alcohol and drug abuse records

These extremely confidential medical records require one of the following:

- A written release by the patient wherein these records are specifically mentioned—not simply "all medical records"
- A court order requiring the records to be released

chapter 15

# Review Questions

## HIPAA and Release of Information

*Indicate whether the sentence or statement is true or false.*

T F 1. The acronym HIPAA represents the Health Insurance Portability and Accountability Act.

T F 2. Breach of confidentiality cannot be charged against a provider if written permission to release necessary medical information to an insurance company or other third party has been obtained from the patient, parent, or guardian.

T F 3. A breach of confidentiality could occur when patient information is communicated to family members without the patient's consent.

T F 4. Confidentiality involves the right of individuals to keep their information from being disclosed to others.

T F 5. The practice should keep a careful log of the transmission of all medically sensitive faxes and copies of all receipt-of-transmittal verifications signed and returned by the authorized recipient.

*Identify the letter of the choice that best completes the statement or answers the question.*

6. Breach of confidentiality can result from:
   a. Sending medical information to other entities without written permission from the patient.
   b. Talking about the patient's case in the business office.
   c. Faxing medical records.
   d. Discussing the patient's health information over the telephone to unauthorized individuals, sending records to unauthorized requestors, or faxing medical records.

7. An authorization signed by the patient is required for release of information to:
   a. Another physician treating the patient.
   b. The patient's health care insurer.
   c. A government agency.
   d. An attorney representing the patient in a civil action.

***Complete each sentence or statement.***

8. Medical practices should keep a dated log of all ______________________________ verification signed and returned by the authorized recipient.

9. Medical practices should routinely review HIPAA policies with all_____________ including ____________.

10. Faxed medical information should be limited to only the information required to __________________________ the immediate needs of the __________________________.

# Answers to Chapter Review Questions

## 1. Gastroenterology

1. A
2. D
3. A
4. C
5. B
6. D
7. B
8. A
9. C
10. D

## 2. Documentation Review

1. T
2. F
3. F
4. T
5. T
6. F
7. SOAP, CHEDDAR
8. Legal document
9. Appropriate for the patient's condition, medically necessary for the diagnosis.

## 3. CPT

1. T
2. T
3. T
4. C
5. D
6. A
7. C
8. C
9. January 1
10. Temporary

## 4. E/M CODING

1. T
2. F
3. F
4. T
5. F
6. A
7. B
8. Detailed, detailed, low
9. Referral, consultation
10. Documentation of request, for an evaluation and opinion, letter back to requesting physician

## 5. Anesthesia

1. T
2. T
3. F
4. General, regional, local
5. (PS) Physical Status, (QC) Qualifying Circumstances

## 6. Surgery

1. T
2. F
3. T
4. F
5. A
6. A
7. Size, number, benign/malignant
8. Diagnostic

## 7. Radiology/ Laboratory

1. T
2. Equipment, radiologic technicians
3. Radiologic views
4. 26

## 8. Medicine

1. T
2. F
3. F
4. T
5. B
6. C
7. D

## 9. Modifiers

1. A
2. D
3. K
4. G
5. L
6. H
7. I
8. D
9. J
10. M
11. N
12. B
13. C
14. E
15. F
16. A

## 10. HCPCS

1. T
2. D
3. D
4. D
5. A
6. C
7. National
8. Temporary National (Non-Medicare)
9. G, K, Q
10. HCPCS National

## 11. ICD-9-CM

1. F
2. F
3. F
4. T
5. C
6. B
7. D
8. Diagnosis
9. Not Elsewhere Classified
10. See Category

## 12. Abstracting

1. B
2. C
3. C
4. B
5. D
6. D
7. B
8. C

## 13. Anatomy/ Terminology

1. D
2. A
3. D
4. C
5. B

## 14. Fraud and Abuse

1. T
2. T
3. T
4. F
5. A
6. C
7. Submission, The medical record documentation, Obtaining
8. Financial
9. Multiple CPT/HCPCS, CPT/HCPCS
10. Compliance Plan

## 15. HIPAA

1. T
2. T
3. T
4. F
5. T
6. D
7. A
8. Receipt of transmittal
9. Staff, physicians
10. Satisfy, requesting party

# Gastroenterology Coding Exercises

Following are eight exercises designed to help GI coders apply the information in the *AGA Institute/PAHCS Gastroenterology Coding Manual*. Each exercise presents the indications for a particular procedure and the procedure performed. After each exercise, space is provided to fill in the appropriate CPT and ICD-9-CM code(s). Answers to the coding exercises appear on pages 131–35.

# Exercise 1

## INDICATIONS FOR PROCEDURE

For colorectal cancer screening, high risk with family history of colon cancer.

## PROCEDURE

After informed consent was obtained, I sedated the patient with Demerol 50 mg and Versed 2 mg, full monitoring with pulse oximetry and EKG and BP monitoring was performed. With the patient in the left lateral decubitous position, the adult colonoscope was inserted after digital exam revealed the rectum to be normal.

Retroversion of the endoscope in the rectum revealed no abnormalities, and the sigmoid was normal appearing. The descending colon and transverse colon were normal; however, in the hepatic flexure area, a small 3 mm polyp was seen and photo documented. It was completely removed with the cold biopsy forceps. Because of severe looping in the sigmoid as well as overdistension of the patient's abdomen with air, the procedure could not be completed past the hepatic flexure. The patient was then subsequently turned onto his back for withdrawal and to afford a different view of the colon on removal of the instrument. No other abnormalities were found.

***CPT:*** ______________________

***ICD-9-CM:*** ______________________

# Exercise 2

## INDICATIONS FOR PROCEDURE

73-year-old male with no GI complaints for colorectal cancer screening, average risk.

## PROCEDURE

Informed consent was obtained and intravenous sedation was given by me with Demerol 50 mg and Versed 3 mg to the point of light sedation. Full cardiac, BP, and pulse oximetry monitoring was carried out. In the left lateral decubitous position, the video colonoscope was introduced into the rectum, and retroflexion revealed small internal hemorrhoids. In the midsigmoid, there was moderated diverticulosis without inflammation. In the transverse colon, a 1.5-cm benign appearing pedunculated polyp was seen and photo documented. It was removed by snare polypectomy and retrieved for pathology. The scope was then inserted into the remainder of the colon, and the cecum and ileocecal valve were reached. Preparation was excellent. The patient was then turned onto his back to give us a different view on withdrawal and no other abnormalities were found. He tolerated the procedure well and was returned to recovery in stable condition.

***CPT:*** ______________________

***ICD-9-CM:*** ______________________

# Exercise 3

## INDICATIONS FOR PROCEDURE

Patient with 14-year history of ulcerative colitis with documentation of complete colon involvement in the past, for surveillance for dysplasia.

## PROCEDURE

Informed consent was obtained. The patient was given 50 mg of Demerol and 3 mg of Versed intravenously and was monitored by blood pressure, EKG, and pulse oximetry. The video colonoscope was inserted in the rectum and advanced under direct vision through the rectosigmoid after retroversion had been carried out. The rectosigmoid had a significant amount of friability and microerosions compatible with mildly active ulcerative colitis. The mucosal markings appeared more normal above 50 cm, and the remainder of the descending colon, transverse, ascending, and cecal areas appeared somewhat atrophic but otherwise normal. The cecal pole was reached, and the ileocecal valve was intubated. The terminal ileum appeared somewhat dilated and was compatible with backwash ileitis.

The scope was then slowly withdrawn from the cecum with four biopsies being taken from the four different quadrants every 10 cm. A total of 48 biopsies were taken and placed in four separate bottles denoting their location in the colon. There were no other abnormalities seen other than those described above. Patient tolerated procedure well and was returned to his room in stable condition. Because of the multiplicity of biopsies, this procedure took three times the average time over a standard colonoscopy with biopsies.

***CPT:*** ______________________

***ICD-9-CM:*** ______________________

# Exercise 4

## INDICATIONS FOR PROCEDURE

History of nausea and vomiting following gastric bypass surgery with abnormal upper GI series suggestive of either ulceration or early fistula formation.

## PROCEDURE

After informed consent was obtained, and the patient was sedated with 50 mg of Demerol and 3 mg of Versed, the endoscope was introduced under direct visualization and advanced to the small bowel. Esophagus was normal. Upon entering the stomach, postsurgical changes were seen. The suture line was clearly visible on retroflexed examination and appeared to be intact. There appeared to be some shallow erosions that were in the healing stage and the mucosa was friable, but no active bleeding was seen. Biopsies were taken. No other abnormalities were seen. The gastrojejunal anastomosis was slightly tight, and with some mild difficulty the endoscope could be pushed through the anastomosis. The luminal diameter of the anastomosis was approximately 8 mm. Just below the gastrojejunal anastomosis, in the small bowel, there appeared to be an offshoot of bowel, immediately distal to the anastomosis. This was intubated and appeared to be a blind loop, but no evidence of friability or fistula formation was seen. The endoscope was then pulled back to the anastomosis and pushed forward into the other loop, and the jejunum itself could be visualized. The endoscope was advanced into the jejunum; no stricture formation was seen.

The endoscope was withdrawn into the stomach. A TTS balloon was advanced through the endoscope and positioned across the anastomosis. Balloon dilation of the anastomosis was performed to 12 mm and then increased to 13.5 mm. No bleeding was seen. The endoscope was then withdrawn. The patient tolerated the procedure well. Postprocedure vital signs were stable, and the patient went to the recovery suite for observation.

***CPT:*** ______________________

***ICD-9-CM:*** ______________________

# Exercise 5

## INDICATIONS FOR PROCEDURE

Chronic pancreatitis, abdominal pain, abnormal CT scan revealing a 6-cm pancreatic pseudocyst.

## PROCEDURE

Informed consent was obtained. The patient received a total of 75 mg of meperidine and 6 mg of midazolam intravenously during the procedure. A side-viewing duodenoscope was passed through the oropharynx into the proximal esophagus and down to the level of the descending duodenum. The major papilla appeared normal. A pancreatogram and cholangiogram were obtained and were normal. No communication of the pancreatic duct with the pseudocyst was apparent. Endoscopic evaluation of esophagus and duodenum were unremarkable. In the stomach, there was an extrinsic-appearing compression of the posterior gastric wall from the adjacent large pseudocyst. Under fluoroscopic guidance, a needle knife incision was made into the posterior gastric wall and a guidewire placed through the needle knife into the pseudocyst. Balloon dilation of the opening was performed over the guidewire, followed by placement of two 10 French double pigtail stents through the fistula into the pseudocyst. The endoscope was withdrawn. The patient tolerated the procedure well and was transferred to the recovery area in stable condition.

***CPT:*** ______________________

***ICD-9-CM:*** ______________________

# Exercise 6

## INDICATIONS FOR PROCEDURE

Jaundice, weight loss, abnormal CT scan.

## PROCEDURE

Informed consent was obtained. The patient received a total of 100 mg Demerol and 3 mg Versed intravenously during the procedure. Examination of the esophagus, stomach, and duodenal bulb was unremarkable. The major papilla was normal in appearance. The cholangiogram and pancreatogram were obtained using a sphincterotome. A narrowed, strictured area was identified in the proximal bile duct. The guidewire was advanced into the proximal bile duct, and a medium-sized sphincterotomy was done without apparent complications. At this point, the sphincterotome was exchanged for a cytobrush, and brushings were obtained from the bile duct stricture. After this, the cytobrush was removed and a 10 French/5 cm straight stent was then advanced over the guidewire and using the standard pushing device. This was placed in good position across the stricture, with free flow of bile noted after placement. The endoscope was then withdrawn. The procedure lasted approximately 1 hour and was well tolerated. The patient was returned to the recovery suite; postprocedure vital signs were stable.

***CPT:*** ______________________

***ICD-9-CM:*** ______________________

# Exercise 7

## INDICATIONS FOR PROCEDURE

Chronic diarrhea and blood in stool, s/p subtotal colectomy for neoplasm.

## MEDICATIONS

Conscious sedation to ensure adequate patient safety and comfort.

## PROCEDURE

Informed consent was obtained. The patient received a total of meperidine 50 mg and midazolam 5 mg. IV push was given in slow incremental doses with continuous monitoring throughout the procedure. The patient was placed in the left lateral decubitus position. The video colonoscope was introduced. The instrument was advanced to the level of the ileocolic anastomosis and into the distal portion of the terminal ileum. The ileocolic anastomosis was seen at 25 cm. The instrument was advanced to a total depth of approximately 38 cm. The examination of the terminal ileum was remarkable for some mild mucosal erythema. No ulcerations or erosions were seen. Multiple biopsies were obtained. The ileocolic anastomosis was seen at 25 cm. This was also remarkable for some mild mucosal erythema and biopsies were obtained. The examination of the distal 25 cm of remaining colon again showed mild mucosal erythema and edema with some obscuring of the mucosal vascular markings. There were no ulcerations noted. No neoplastic change was seen. Biopsies were obtained at 18 cm and from the distal rectum. Retroflexion view of the rectum on withdrawal showed no other changes.

***CPT:*** ______________________

***ICD-9-CM:*** ______________________

# Exercise 8

## INDICATIONS FOR PROCEDURE

74-year-old female with positive hemoccult, possible mass in left epigastrium, and family history of colon carcinoma.

## PROCEDURE

After informed consent was obtained, with full pulse oximetry and cardiac and BP monitoring, I gave IV sedation to the point of light sedation. Demerol 50 mg and Versed 3 mg was initially administered with another 3 mg Versed during the procedure. With the patient in the left lateral decubitous position, digital exam revealed a normal rectum without masses. The adult video-colonoscope was inserted, and retroversion in the rectum revealed small internal hemorrhoids. The scope was then advanced to the high sigmoid where severe diverticulosis was encountered. The angulation was such that despite multiple manipulations, we were unable to advance the instrument beyond 35 cm. We then finally withdrew the instrument and reinserted the pediatric colonoscope with variable stiffener cables. Again, despite multiple manipulations of the endoscope and the patient's position, we were still not able to advance the instrument safely. Finally, this instrument was withdrawn and a gastrocope was utilized. With this instrument we were able to advance beyond the initial severe angulation but became impacted at 60 cm just below the splenic flexure, whereupon a large obstructing tumor mass was seen. Photos and biopsies were taken. The patient was not a candidate for stenting. Because of the multiple endoscopes used and the prolongation of the procedure to three times that of the standard colonoscopy/biopsy procedure, further sedation was necessitated. The procedure was then terminated with the patient being returned to recovery in stable condition.

***CPT:*** ______________________

***ICD-9-CM:*** ______________________

# Answers to Gastroenterology Coding Exercises

## Exercise 1

| | | |
|---|---|---|
| ***CPT:*** | **45380** | Colonoscopy, flexible proximal to splenic flexure, with biopsy, single or multiple |

***Rationale for code selection:*** The removal of a polyp using cold biopsy forceps is coded as a biopsy. Despite the fact the colonoscopy was not completed to the cecum, it was passed beyond the splenic flexure and thus fits the description for using a colonoscopy code.

| | | |
|---|---|---|
| ***ICD-9-CM:*** | **V16.0** | Family history of malignant neoplasm of gastrointestinal tract |
| | **211.3** | Benign neoplasm of colon |

***Rationale for code selection:*** Only code when pathology report confirms that polyp was benign. If coding prior to the receipt of the pathology report, use 235.2 Neoplasm of uncertain behavior.

***Coding tip:*** When coding procedures and the procedure performed is fully described by an existing CPT code, use that CPT code. If the procedure is not accurately described by the code, then use the miscellaneous code 44799, Unlisted procedure, intestine, and submit by paper claim using comparisons to the nearest known CPT-described procedure for payment comparisons.

## Exercise 2

| | | |
|---|---|---|
| ***CPT:*** | **45385** | Colonoscopy, flexible, proximal to splenic flexure with removal of tumor(s), polyp(s), or other lesion(s) by snare technique |

| | | |
|---|---|---|
| ***ICD-9-CM:*** | **V76.51** | Screening for malignant neoplasm of colon |
| | **211.3** | Benign neoplasm of colon |
| | **562.10** | Diverticulosis |

***Rational for code selection:*** Although the indication for the procedure was a colonoscopy for colorectal cancer screening, average risk, the procedure that was performed was a colonoscopy with snare polypectomy. You should then use as the first diagnosis ICD-9-CM code V76.51 Screening for CRC, with the second diagnosis code being 211.3 Benign neoplasm of the colon, and the third diagnosis, 562.10 for colonic diverticulosis. Put a 2 in box 24E to link polypectomy with polyp.

If no polyp had been found, despite the finding of diverticulosis, the proper procedure code would have been the G0121 using the V diagnosis for CRC screening, ICD-9-CM V76.51 Special screening for malignant neoplasm, colon, with colonic diverticulosis as the second ICD-9-CM code.

***Coding tip:*** Although the directive to convert a screening colonoscopy to diagnostic or therapeutic colonoscopy when there are significant findings comes directly from CMS, the instructions to maintain the original diagnosis as primary even when there are significant findings, for all other endoscopic procedures, may vary by insurance company.

Unfortunately, not all payers recognize the G codes for colorectal cancer screening, nor is colorectal cancer screening a covered benefit under all insurance plans. Contact the insurance company to determine coverage and their specific method of coding for the procedure.

## Exercise 3

| ***CPT:*** | **45380-22** | Colonoscopy, flexible, proximal to splenic flexure with biopsy single or multiple with unusual procedure modifier |
|---|---|---|

***Rationale for code selection:*** Although the CPT code descriptor says single or multiple biopsies, the unusual number of biopsies required for ulcerative colitis surveillance for dysplasia requires an inordinate amount of time over that of the standard colonoscopy with biopsies. Therefore, it would be appropriate for the 22 modifier to be appended to the standard code and the claim to be submitted for paper review.

| ***ICD-9-CM:*** | **556.1** | Ulcerative (chronic) ileocolitis |
|---|---|---|

***Coding tip:*** When using the 22 modifier, it is important to document the number of biopsies as well as the amount of time spent during the procedure as compared to the more typical procedure to allow for appropriate reimbursement for your additional work

## Exercise 4

| ***CPT:*** | **43245** | Esophagogastroduodenoscopy with dilation of gastric outlet for obstruction |
|---|---|---|
| | **43239** | Esophagogastroduodenoscopy with biopsy |

***Rationale for code selection:*** The CMS policy allows for the billing of multiple procedures performed during the same endoscopy. The Medicare payment is based on the full value of the highest valued endoscopy plus the difference between the next highest, and so forth, and the base endoscopy. The base endoscopy is generally the diagnostic endoscopy that is the first code in the group.

| | | |
|---|---|---|
| ***ICD-9-CM:*** | **564.3** | Vomiting following gastrointestinal surgery |
| | **997.4** | Digestive systems complications |

***Coding tip:*** The 51 modifier for multiple surgical procedures does not apply to endoscopies. Bill the full fee for each procedure. The payer will apply the appropriate discount and the difference between the fee charged, and the allowed amount would be written off as a contractual adjustment, if appropriate.

# Exercise 5

| | | |
|---|---|---|
| ***CPT:*** | **43260** | Endoscopic retrograde cholangiopancreatography (ERCP); diagnostic, with or without collection of specimen(s) by brushing or washing (separate procedure) |
| | **43240** | Upper gastrointestinal endoscopy including esophagus, stomach, and either the duodenum and/or jejunum as appropriate; with transmural drainage of pseudocyst |

***Rationale for code selection:*** If multiple procedures are being performed during the same endoscopic examination, they should be billed separately.

| | | |
|---|---|---|
| ***ICD-9-CM:*** | **577.2** | Pseudocyst of pancreas |
| | **577.1** | Chronic pancreatitis |
| | **793.4** | Abnormal findings, GI tract |
| | **789.00** | Abdominal pain, unspecified. |

***Coding tip:*** The balloon dilation, stent placement, and the use of fluoroscopic guidance are performed as components of the pseudocyst drainage and are included in the physician work component of code 43240. Code 43260 may be rejected by the insurance carrier as included in 43240. However, as 43240 involved significantly more work than 43260 performed alone, if rejected, the claim should be resubmitted for manual review.

# Exercise 6

| | | |
|---|---|---|
| ***CPT:*** | **43262** | ERCP with sphincterotomy/papillotomy |
| | **43268** | ERCP with endoscopic retrograde insertion of tube or stent into bile or pancreatic duct |

***Rationale for code selection:*** The CMS policy allows for the billing of multiple procedures performed during the same endoscopy. The Medicare payment is based on the full value of the highest valued endoscopy plus the difference between the next highest, and so forth, and the base endoscopy. The base endoscopy is generally the diagnostic endoscopy that is the first code in the group. Brushings are included in the description of 43260 and cannot be separately billed. If a specific biopsy other than brushing had been performed, 43261 could have been billed.

| | | |
|---|---|---|
| ***ICD-9-CM:*** | **576.2** | Obstruction of bile duct |
| | **782.4** | Jaundice |

| | |
|---|---|
| **783.21** | Loss of weight |
| **793.3** | Abnormal findings, biliary tract |

***Coding tip:*** The 51 modifier for multiple surgical procedures does not apply to endoscopies. Bill the full fee for each procedure. The payer will apply the appropriate discount and the difference between the fee charged, and the allowed amount would be written off as a contractual adjustment, if appropriate.

## Exercise 7

***CPT:*** **45380** Colonoscopy, flexible, proximal to splenic flexure with biopsy, single or multiple

***Rationale for code selection:*** Although multiple biopsies were taken, the code can only be billed once.

| | | |
|---|---|---|
| ***ICD-9-CM:*** | **578.1** | Blood in stool |
| | **564.5** | Diarrhea, functional |
| | **569.89** | Other specified condition of the intestine |

***Coding tips:*** If the biopsies were so extensive as to require significantly more time than an average procedure, you can append the 22 modifier. The claim must be submitted with the procedure report as well as a short statement indicating the complexity of the procedure and the additional time it took to perform. The 22 modifier should only be used when the expectation of increased reimbursement is significant, as the claim will require manual review and may take several months for processing.

## Exercise 8

***CPT:*** **45380-52, -22** Colonoscopy with biopsy, 52 modifier for incomplete colonoscopy with full preparation, and 22 modifier to signify an unusual, prolonged procedure

***Rationale for code selection:*** The CMS policy for an incomplete colonoscopy is to append the 53 modifier. However, Medicare payment for this procedure is based on the reimbursement for a flexible sigmoidoscopy. As a flexible sigmoidoscopy does not contain the work value for moderate (conscious) sedation, you can attach the 22 modifier to signify the additional work, time, and effort sometimes required for an incomplete colonoscopy, as Medicare does not pay for moderate (conscious) sedation when administered by the same provider that performed the endoscopic procedure. CPT rules are to use the 52 modifier and submit documentation by paper report as to the additional time, effort, and risk associated with the procedure.

| | | |
|---|---|---|
| ***ICD-9-CM:*** | **455.0** | Neoplasm of uncertain behavior |
| | **792.1** | Occult blood |
| | **455.0** | Internal hemorrhoids |
| | **562.10** | Diverticulosis |

***Rationale for code selection:*** Do not code the tumor as malignant until the pathology report confirms that fact. Code abnormal findings in the order of severity.

***Coding tip:*** The 22 modifier should only be used when the expectation of increased reimbursement is significant, as the claim will require manual review and may take several months for processing.

# Resources

### *American Gastroenterological Association (AGA) Institute*

4930 Del Ray Avenue
Bethesda, MD 20814
301-654-2055
Fax: 301-652-3890
www.gastro.org

### *Professional Association of Healthcare Coding Specialists*

218 East Bearss Avenue, #354
Tampa, FL 33613
888-708-4704
Fax: 813-333-1596
www.pahcs.org

### *Centers for Medicare and Medicaid Services (CMS)*

P.O. Box 26688
Baltimore, MD 21207-0488
www.cms.hhs.gov
Download E/M Documentation Guidelines from:
http://www.cms.hhs.gov/MLNEdwebguide/25_EMDOC.asp

### *Office of Inspector General (OIG)*

Department of Health and Human Services
330 Independence Avenue, SW
Washington, DC 20201
www.hhs.gov

# Index of CPT Codes

# Index of Topics